You Ma...
Quantum Leap Fan
But Did You Know That . . .

Many of Sam's leapees believe they have been abducted by aliens?

The episode that aired on halloween in 1990 is considered haunted, and is associated with a record number of local station/cable/VCR failures?

The ratings rose three points when Sam took off his shirt for two consecutive acts?

Sam can die when he has "leapt" into another person?

Project Quantum Leap has cost the taxpayers $43 billion?

Look for

TREK: THE UNAUTHORIZED A-Z
by Hal Schuster and Wendy Rathbone

THE UNAUTHORIZED HISTORY OF *TREK*
by James Van Hise

THE UNAUTHORIZED TREKKERS' GUIDE TO *THE NEXT GENERATION* AND *DEEP SPACE NINE*
by James Van Hise

SCI FI TV: FROM *THE TWILIGHT ZONE* TO *DEEP SPACE NINE*
by James Van Hise

STAR TREK MEMORIES
by William Shatner with Chris Kreski

STAR TREK MOVIE MEMORIES
by William Shatner with Chris Kreski

Published by HarperPrism

The Making of

QUANTUM LEAP

HAL SCHUSTER

HarperPrism
An Imprint of HarperPaperbacks

This is a work of fiction. The characters, incidents, and dialogues are products of the author's imagination and are not to be construed as real. Any resemblance to actual events or persons, living or dead, is entirely coincidental.

HarperPaperbacks *A Division of* HarperCollins*Publishers*
10 East 53rd Street, New York, N.Y. 10022

Copyright © 1996 by Pioneer Books, Inc.
All rights reserved. No part of this book may be used or reproduced in any manner whatsoever without written permission of the publisher, except in the case of brief quotations embodied in critical articles and reviews. For information address HarperCollins*Publishers,*
10 East 53rd Street, New York, N.Y. 10022.

A trade paperback edition of this book was published by Pioneer Books, Inc.

Cover photograph of Scott Bakula by Michael Grecco/Sygma
Background cover art by L. Manning/Westlight

First HarperPrism printing: April 1996
Printed in the United States of America

HarperPrism is an imprint of HarperPaperbacks.
HarperPaperbacks, HarperPrism, and colophon are trademarks of HarperCollins*Publishers.*

❖ 10 9 8 7 6 5 4 3 2 1

Contents

Acknowledgments

I would like to thank Pamela Ashworth, Debbie Brown, Margaret Colchin, Jason Dzembo, Ailsa Jenkins, Anita Kilgour, Scott Nance, Shari Ramseur, Sally Smith, Ava Webster, and Kitty Woldow, Leapers extraordinary. Sally Smith helped me far above and beyond the call of duty. I would also like to thank Caitlin Deinard Blasdell for her kind assistance.

Introduction

With great pleasure, I now lay computer to rest after completing this book dedicated to the best and most popular television series about time travel ever aired. It is also the most literate, far surpassing earlier efforts, such as Irwin Allen's fondly remembered *Time Tunnel*.

Time travel, the ability to move through time and witness historical events, or even our own future, fascinates humankind. Perhaps the modern preoccupation began in 1895 with H. G. Wells's celebrated novel *Time Machine*, which was filmed many times. It has continued in movies and TV series as well as countless novels and short stories, such as Ray Bradbury's "The Sound of Thunder," in which a man ventures back to primordial days and accidentally steps upon and kills an insect, irrevocably changing his own modern world. As I write this introduction, the BBC news has just announced that Stephen Hawking, possibly the best known modern British scientist, now believes time travel to be possible due to a combination of Einstein's theorems and quantum physics. This reverses his previous statements.

Quantum Leap didn't worry too much about such niceties. The series offered a quick explanation and let it go at that, preferring to concentrate on meaningful stories and characters endowed with humanity and heroism. In this book we touch on many aspects of the show, brought to life by a gifted staff and actors. I hope you enjoy what follows for a very long time.

Hal Schuster
Bangkok, October 2, 1995

1

Project *Quantum Leap:* A Series Primer

by Debbie Brown

Project *Quantum Leap* is a high-security project located in a cavern in New Mexico in 1995 (when the show started; it now seems to be 1999). So far it's cost $43 billion of our tax dollars, with an additional cost of $2.4 billion annually for operating funds. It began with just Sam and Al "raising the funding, poring over the blueprints late at night," and listening to the score of *Man of La Mancha*.

Viewers never learn what the Project was supposed to do, other than allow Sam to time-travel within his own lifetime; we do learn that Sam leaped too soon (before everything was ready, when the government was threatening to cut funding). Apparently God (or fate or time or some other unfathomable force—like maybe Don Bellisario?) decided to use Sam to "put things right that once went wrong."

The Project is built around Sam and Al's brain waves. When he leaps, Sam actually possesses the new host body in the past, while the mind of the host travels into the future, to keep things even. The host's aura is what people see; Sam only knows who he's leaped into when he looks in the mirror, and is forever figuring out whom he's replaced and what good deed he's there to do. Sam's the only guy who can figure out how to get himself back home, but the first leap completely Swiss-cheesed his memory (technical term is "magnafluxed"). Under normal conditions, Sam's the only person who can see and hear Al, although animals, people on the verge of death, the "mentally absent," and children under five always can; they also see Sam as himself. Al appears to Sam through a "neurological hologram" process: "agitated carbon quarks tuned to the optic and otic neurons." Al sees Sam as the leapee, but always knows who he is.

Sam

Sam (Dr. Samuel Beckett, no relation to the playwright) was born in 1953. He grew up on his family's dairy farm, in Elk Ridge, Indiana. As a child, he had two cats, Donner and Blitzen, but never a dog. He could read at the age of two, do advanced calculus in his head at five, and went to MIT at fifteen, graduating two years later. He holds six doctorates in fields including medicine, quantum physics, and ancient languages, but not in psychiatry or law. He speaks seven modern languages including English, Japanese, French, Spanish, and German, but not Italian or Hebrew, and four dead ones (he can read Egyptian hieroglyphics). He has won a Nobel Prize, field unspecified, but probably for physics. For this, *Time* magazine called him "the next Einstein."

He played the piano at Carnegie Hall at nineteen, plays guitar, is a good dancer, and sings tenor (his favorite song is John Lennon's "Imagine"). He possesses a photographic memory, can cook, and likes dry or light beer and microwave popcorn. Sam also practices several martial arts, but has been afraid of heights since he was nine years old. He was engaged once, but believed himself stood up at the altar. An accident occurred during a leap in the middle of a lightning storm that caused Sam and Al temporarily to change places. At this time he discovered he wasn't stood up at the altar, but was in fact married to his greatest love, Donna. This was due to events in a prior leap when he was able to alter her life so that she could commit to marriage with him.

Sam's older brother, Tom, was an All-State basketball player, Annapolis grad, and navy SEAL, who convinced Sam to go to MIT. Tom died in Vietnam, on April 8, 1970. Sam saved him on one leap. Their father, John, died in 1974 of a heart attack. Sam has one sister named Katie (Katherine), born during a flood in 1957, whose first husband was an abusive alcoholic named Chuck. Now she's married to a navy officer, Lieutenant Jim Bonnick, and lives in Hawaii with their mother, Thelma.

Al

When Rear Admiral Albert Calavicci was a child, his part-Russian mom ran off with an encyclopedia salesman. Al's father, an Italian immigrant—Al speaks fluent Italian—was a construction worker; when he went to the Middle East, Al was sent to an orphanage, and his retarded sister, Trudy, to an institution. Later his father and his father's girl-friend often spirited him out of the orphanage. Al often ran away; once he joined the circus, and once he spent several months traveling with a pool wizard. He had a pet cockroach named Kevin and a dog named Chester (of whom he lost custody to his third wife). While in the orphanage, Al took up acting and also fought Golden Gloves. When he was old enough, he went to get his sister, but she'd died of pneumonia in the institution in 1953 at age sixteen.

During the sixties, Al went on civil-rights marches. Later Al went to MIT, joined the navy, and became a pilot. From 1968 to 1973 he was a prisoner of the Viet Cong; during this time his first wife, Beth, a navy nurse, lost hope, had him declared dead, and married a lawyer. Later, he became an astronaut and is now a "highly respected and decorated" rear admiral. He likes and collects sports cars and classic cars. Al watches sports, gambles a little (takes trips to Las Vegas and bets on horse races), and, in the past, had a tendency to drink to excess. Al met Sam on the Starbright Project (which is never explained); when they first met, Al was drunk and beating up on a vending machine with a hammer. Sam's influence kept Al from being removed from the project because of his drinking. Al's association with Sam helped sober him up.

This is all secondary to Al's main interest—women! He's been married five times; his first, third, and fifth honeymoons were spent on trains to Niagara Falls. Wife #3, Ruthie, was Jewish; #4 was Sharon ("she wore pink babydolls"); he met #5, named Maxine ("she didn't wear anything at all—she used to flavor her toes with mint leaves"), in a tattoo parlor. Either his second or third wife was Hungarian. Currently, Al semiregularly dates a blonde named Tina (they met in Vegas) who has a pet crocodile and a tattoo in a "super-private part of her anatomy." Although Al firmly believes in the "double standard," he respects women as individuals and gets very angry when they're mistreated. Al dresses flashy, smokes a lot of cigars, is somewhat superstitious, has a serious aversion to dead bodies, and possesses a great recipe for chitlins.

Ziggy and Gooshie

Gooshie (played by Dennis Wolfberg) is Ziggy's programmer/operator and operates the imaging chamber that projects Al's image back to Sam. He's the one Al sometimes talks to, a "short guy with bad breath" and a mustache. Tina once went to Vegas for a weekend with him just to make Al jealous. It worked. Ziggy says he's having an affair with Tina.

Ziggy is the Project's "parallel hybrid computer," created by Sam. Ziggy has a definite personality: a big ego, crashes a lot, hates to be wrong, and frequently sulks! He freaks out sometimes, too—once he turned off the climate control, once he wouldn't output in anything but Japanese, and once he stuck an extra zero on the end of everyone's paycheck, leaving Al to report that "half the staff took off on vacation!"

That's the way it appeared until September of 1991. Then, in the fourth-season opener, Ziggy was revealed to be a she. The influence of Sam's wife, Donna, may have given Ziggy a female identity, a perfect example of Sam's changes catching up with them. Ziggy responds to queries with a female voice (Deborah Pratt's), and may be the narrator of the saga that opens the show each week.

2

Frequently Asked *QL* Questions

by Debbie Brown

This chapter answers the most frequently asked questions about *Quantum Leap*. It also attempts to catalog the information viewers have been able to glean from individual stories and other, official and nonofficial, sources.

1. Who controls the leaps?

Nobody knows. Sam and Al know that it's not Ziggy or anyone at Project Quantum Leap. Al told Sam in the pilot episode that Sam's leaps were out of the Project's control, so Sam and Al hypothesize that it's Him (eyes heavenward) who is controlling things.

2. When Al looks at Sam, what does he see?

Al sees the leapee. In the episode entitled "What

Price, Gloria?" Al lost control at seeing Sam as a gorgeous secretary. Al probably recognizes Sam because they are linked through their brain-wave transmissions, which is what the Project uses to locate Sam in time.

3. Who is in the "waiting room"?

The leapee. To everyone at the Project, the leapee looks like Sam. In one episode, the leapee was someone Al knew, since Al recognized him in the waiting room. We don't know if Al just recognized the personality or if this was a gaffe on the part of the writers. Don Bellisario has described the waiting room as a sterile, hospital-like room where the leapee is examined by the Project's medical staff. Once we got to see (and hear) the leapee when she entered the imaging chamber with Al, and she looked to us like the image Sam saw in the mirror. This is probably due to the same mechanism that allows us to see Sam as Sam.

4. When Sam looks at himself, what does he see?

He sees himself, Sam Beckett—unless he looks into a mirror. Then he sees the leapee.

5. Can anyone else at the Project go into the imaging chamber and see Sam?

Depends. In one episode, "Star-Crossed," several committee members entered the chamber with Al, but for them, they were in an empty room with Al talking to thin air. The others were not visible to Sam (or us). Only when Al is touching an object will it be visible to Sam (and us). In more than one episode, Al brought an object into the waiting room for Sam to see (this is beyond Al's clothing and cigar). Skin-to-skin contact is needed for another person to be seen in the imaging chamber. Dr. Beeks, by holding Al's hand, appeared to be able to see Sam and in turn was seen by him (and us).

6. Can Sam die during a leap?

According to Don Bellisario, he can.

7. Why could Sam see when he "replaced" a blind man? Would he be able to hear as a deaf person?

It appears that Sam physically leaps through time, his mass being exchanged with that of the leapee. Sam, not sharing the handicap, will not exhibit it. (The part about Sam physically leaping through time could change should the BGU decide "he wants it that way.")

According to Don Bellisario, "When Sam leaps in and bounces somebody out, I like to think of it this way: If that person was hit by a car and they broke their leg and hit the street and then Sam leaped in, Sam would not have a broken leg. But if Sam leaped in and was crossing the street and was hit by the car, then Sam would have the broken leg."

In other words, he does not share handicaps or injuries suffered by the leapee before his leap in, but will sustain injuries suffered after the leap. We don't know if Sam will still have this injury during his next leap, or if the leapee in the waiting room will suffer the injury when he or she gets back. Whether the leapee will exhibit any of Sam's injuries while they are in the waiting room isn't known either.

8. What does the leapee remember about his experience after he returns?

This, too, is not known. The only time we've seen this occur was in the episode "Double Identity," in which Sam leaped to replace another body and the original host returned. He appeared to have no memory of anything after he was leaped into. However, we don't think this is the normal effect, since this leap was generated by Ziggy in an attempt to retrieve Sam. It has been stated that the leapee, while in Sam's body back in the waiting room, has a "Swiss-cheesed" memory, much like Sam received upon his initial leap. Because of the ultramodern hospitallike atmosphere of the waiting room, many of the leapees believe they have been abducted by aliens.

9. Can anyone see Sam as Sam, rather than as the leapee? Can anyone other than Sam see Al?

Small children, the "mentally absent," animals, and people near death can see him. (And pretty blondes with low IQs if Al got his way.) Al has explained that children and animals see things as they really are because they exist in a natural alpha state. Also, if a person's brain waves were sufficiently in tune with Sam's, that person would be able to see and hear Al, too.

10. Why can't Sam leap back beyond his own lifetime (or, why can't he leap into the far past)?

This is all part of Sam Beckett's "string theory." A person's lifetime is like a string—one end of the string is one's birth; the other end, death. Tie the ends together and ball up the string, and all the days of a lifetime touch all the other days of a lifetime. If someone can loosen himself from the string, he can quantum-leap from one day to the any other. On one occasion (so far) Sam was able to leap back to a time before the date of his birth due to an accident that occurred during a leap out in the middle of a thunderstorm. Al and Sam leaped together and wound up trading places. Al in the past, Sam in the future. This dual leap caused an exchange of subatomic matter between Al and Sam, allowing Sam to leap back into Al in the year 1945. It isn't known at this time if this exchange of matter will be permanent (therefore allowing Sam to leap even further back) or if it was cleared up when Sam leaped back.

11. What would happen if Sam failed to do what he was sent to do?

Again, nobody knows. One theory is that he would be trapped in the past forever, replacing the host. This, however, is doubtful. Another theory is that he would leap into another's life to attempt again to fix "that which has gone wrong." In "Double Identity," Sam was pulled from the leapee by Ziggy without resolving the problem he was sent to fix. He leaped immediately to replace another body in the same room and in that second body completed his mission.

12. How does Ziggy know so much about people's lives in the past?

Ziggy is hooked up to every major database of the midnineties. It's amazing, when you think about it, just how much information about you is stored on computers.

13. How is it that when Sam leaps into a leapee who is shorter/smaller than he is, people around him don't notice a difference in size?

It's a question of topology. Consider the following argument: The QL maps everything from a different time into a frame of reference relative to Sam. (And vice versa for the host.) Sam doesn't see what really happens, but rather what happens relative to his host.

It's all a matter of relativity as well. Consider a spaceship ten meters long. Send it off at 99.4 percent of the speed of light and it will seem to be only one meter long to anyone still on Earth, while still seeming to be ten meters long to those on board. Gravity can do the same sort of thing; put an object deep into a gravity well and it will seem shorter. The ship is in a different "reference frame" than the Earth, and the object in the well is in a different frame than the observer floating outside it, and things like length (also duration) are not the same across reference frames.

So here's the theory: When Sam leaps, his whole body leaps, but it is mapped into a different reference frame. If you look through a warped piece of glass, things seem to be a different size and shape. The same thing happens with a warped region of space. When Sam leaps, the space containing him is warped in such a way that not just length, but all physical properties are altered. And, of course, the only person in Sam's reference frame is Sam, so when he looks at himself, he sees what he has always seen, but when he looks in a mirror, the photons have passed between frames, and so he sees the leapee.

To answer the original question, when Sam, six feet tall or so, has leaped into someone five-foot-seven and is talking to someone, they look at the leapee's eyes, he sees them looking at his eyes, and likewise he looks down, but the person he's talking to sees the leapee looking straight. Which is really right? Neither, or both! It's the same as asking "How long is the spaceship really?" The answer is completely dependent on what frame you're in because certain physical properties have no absolute existence.

As for how this ties into super-strings: Current thought is that strings don't just define particles, but also in some sense define space and time. When Sam leaps, he takes the strings composing his body and "soul" into a region of space made up of the strings of the person he's replacing.

14. What is the imaging chamber?

This is the only place where Al can go to talk to Sam. Its construction allows a holographic image of Al to be generated for transmission into Sam's optic and auditory neurons in the past, and for Sam and his surrounding images to be projected onto Al's neurons. Speculation has it that this is a very large and cavernous room judging from the amount of walking Al can do without bumping into walls and the sound of the door as it slides open and closed.

15. What about other inconsistencies in *QL*?

"Don't investigate this too closely."—Don Bellisario, March 17, 1990.

16. I have a script I wrote for the show. How do I get it to the producers?

One word: Don't. Really. Sally Smith reports, "The producers have specifically asked that no scripts be sent in," and says they do not even look at unsolicited scripts, not even those submitted by professional writers. Despite the fact that they do not use other people's ideas, lawsuits are still filed against them. People assume that if they send in a script and something similar shows up in a story, they were ripped off, even though their script was never read by anyone at the company. Think of it this way: If you thought of it, they've probably thought of it, too, and can either do it better, are already in the process of doing it, or have already discarded the idea.

Writer-producer Chris Ruppenthal says, "Hey, that's a good question. That's a terrifying question. Quite frankly, stories are submitted only through agents accredited with the Writers' Guild of America, East or West. We cannot—even if you call up on the phone, and say, 'Hey, I don't want any money for this'—which a lot of people do. It's unfortunate, but the way the legal system is today, and what has happened to us in the past, we have to be very strict and very certain. If you submit a manuscript, a *Quantum Leap* spec script, it will be returned unread by our legal department. We just can't. What we don't want to do to aspiring writers, or writers who've already done some work, is consciously or unconsciously co-opt an idea and beat you out of the money. Because it's only fair that your ideas get the recognition they deserve, if they're good ideas, and the payment they deserve, they have to go through an agent. And not an attorney, but an agent, a literary agent, who can represent you."

If you really want to break into the business, *Star Trek: The Next Generation* does accept unsolicited scripts.

17. Who is this "Gooshie" that Al keeps talking to?

Gooshie is Ziggy's programmer, a short guy with bad breath. He used to be shown very briefly in profile, wearing a headset in the opening title sequence as Sam is leaping out and in for the episode "The Leap Back."

18. What are "Leapheads"?

There is no such creature as a Leaphead. This is a word coined by an NBC employee referring to a Leaper, which is a *Quantum Leap* fan. "Leaper" is the preferred term, used by the fans themselves and the cast and crew of *Quantum Leap* when speaking about the fans. The prevailing attitude is: If "Leaper" is good enough for Don Bellisario and company, it's good enough for us.

19. So what's the story with that episode titled "The B**giem*n" and why do Leapers refuse to mention it by name?

This episode first aired near Halloween 1990, and from then on, weird events have been associated with it. For example, airings of this episode coincide with the highest incidence of VCR/cable/local-station failure. There have been numerous reports of VCRs cutting out during the taping of this episode, and of local stations and cable companies dropping their signal. Even mentioning it by name is hazardous, as one Leaper can attest. This hapless individual—who knew better—was bandying about the name of this episode. He lost his job. Its mention has been known to cause power failures and auto breakdowns, so it's best just to refer to it as "The Halloween Episode." Leapers everywhere will know of what you speak.

By the way, cameras and recording equipment also tend to act strangely around Chris Ruppenthal, the writer of this episode. Since it aired, his nickname has been "Ruppenboogie." He is kind enough not to say the title of the episode around the fans, though director Joe Napolitano does.

20. Is Scott Bakula really as nice as he seems?

Yes, yes, a thousand times yes. A perfect example of just how nice, patient, hardworking, and decent is his appearance at the *QL* screening for the fans in L.A. back on February 25, 1991. He had put in a hard day on the set, working on the episode "Last Dance Before an Execution," a very emotionally intense, demanding script, when he had to appear at the screening to answer questions (with the BGU, Deborah Pratt and Dean) and meet the fans. He was pleasant and open, even joking with people and accepting small gifts and hugs with aplomb.

Afterward he was mobbed by (literally!) hundreds of

mostly female fans who requested his autograph and to have their picture taken with him. He spoke to each person and smiled for the cameras. He is truly a sweet, gracious person, traits that are shared by the rest of the people associated with this production.

21. I remember watching a time-travel show in the sixties, *Time Tunnel*. Anyone else remember it?

Ah yes, Irwin Allen's *Time Tunnel*. This was a show about a secret government-funded time-travel experiment in which a young researcher sends himself back in time in an effort to prevent the project's funding from being cut. This, the two men traveling through time, and the efforts to retrieve them are the only things the show has in common with *Quantum Leap*, which only has one man traveling through time, his companion firmly rooted in the future. On *Time Tunnel*, time travelers Anthony Newman and Dough Phillips unfailingly arrived at historical events and desperately tried to influence outcomes based on their knowledge of the future. They always failed. The time travelers would find themselves in the Roman Colosseum one week, and in Napoleon's army the next, then tripping off to the bombing of Pearl Harbor. It is drastic time changes like this that Don Bellisario wanted to avoid when he imposed the "within his own lifetime" rule. He felt the huge differences in time settings were distracting and unrealistic.

22. Isn't *Quantum Leap* just like that other time travel show, *Voyagers*?

Phineas Bogg and his companion, Jeffrey Jones, are

time travelers who find themselves trying to fix history, or to "put things right" when "people become displaced in time and find themselves a half-step away from a total different destiny." In one episode, Franklin D. Roosevelt became a movie director and it was up to Phineas and Jeffrey to set him on the right course to the presidency of the United States. This show found its heroes traveling to far-flung places and times, a plot device Don Bellisario wanted to avoid.

23. If Al is a hologram, why does he cast shadows?

The shadows are holograms, too, and are generated and projected by Ziggy as part of the process, of course. Seriously, while Al may not cast shadows, Dean certainly does (especially since—as Michael Watkins once put it—"Dean likes to talk with his hands so much that he's a pretty active shadow anyway"). It's simply physically impossible to eliminate them all. Also, there are times when having Al not cast a shadow would actually make him look fake, like a pasted-on cutout effect instead of a real person.

3

Project *Quantum Leap:* Making Time Travel Look Easy

Don Bellisario has a lot in common with Sam Beckett. Both of them embark on a project that seems as if it can never work. For Beckett, the problem is physics; for Bellisario, networks and ratings. It has been a labor of love for both. They both have fought hard to keep their projects alive; Beckett's, the fictional time-travel experiment, and Bellisario's, the very real television experiment that has given the medium one more show of substance.

Bellisario, whose other television hit credits include *Magnum, P.I.* and *Airwolf*, had completed a feature film, *Last Rites*, and wanted his next project to be a change of pace. He recalls, "The film was very dark in tone and had a dark, downer ending to it and so I decided that for my next project, I wanted to do something up, that I could have fun with. I knew I didn't want to do what had been done before, which was primarily straight action/adventure stuff."

Producing a No-No

Bellisario also wanted to produce a "network no-no," an anthology program, like *The Twilight Zone* or *Alfred Hitchcock Presents*. "My initial thought was, 'Wouldn't it be nice to do something that is a four-letter word to networks and studios?' which is an anthology show," he says. "Then I started figuring out how you make an anthology show that does well. Obviously, I needed recurring characters who people would like and tune in every week to see. The problem was how to do an anthology show with the same central characters."

A book Bellisario had recently read, *Coming of Age in the Milky Way*, suggested the idea of time travel, which set the producer in the right direction. TV had seen other time-travel sagas filled with ideas Bellisario didn't like. He says, "I used to hate it when the guy would pop up on a Phoenician sailing ship one week and in Napoleon's army the next. That was all very unreal to me."

The networks were predictably reluctant. Bellisario had to tailor the concept of time travel to make it more "believable"—a whole set of rules had to be constructed. Finally, NBC was convinced. Bellisario said, "I told them that the central character would not be able to leap beyond his own lifetime. I further told them since the show's theory was that the universe was finite and that matter could not be added to or subtracted from a given period, that any era Sam leaps into, he would have to bounce somebody out and take their place.

"Then I told them I wouldn't materialize Sam in the middle of a major historical event each week and that

Sam's brain would be 'Swiss-cheesed' every episode so he couldn't remember what was happening. I threw in Al the hologram to go along as a sidekick, and bingo, I had the series."

Casting Travelers

At that point Bellisario may have had the groundwork for a series, but the series itself was yet to come. Enter the actors Scott Bakula as Sam and veteran Dean Stockwell as the holographic sidekick. "*Quantum Leap* came across my agent's desk and then to me," explains Bakula. "I liked the material so much I just said, 'Let's do it!' Since then, the worry has always been, 'Will NBC give us enough time to find an audience?' They've been great about it. They hung in with us last year. They renewed us. We didn't jump out of the gate like crazy this year. What we've done, very slowly and gradually, is build a pretty solid audience for NBC in our Wednesday at ten o'clock slot. My past experience has always been not getting support from our network. That's not a problem here."

"The concept and the writing of the pilot sold itself to me," recalls Dean Stockwell. "Plus the track record of the producer, Donald P. Bellisario, who had produced and created *Magnum*, *Airwolf*, and *Tales of the Gold Monkey*—all of them good shows. Also the fact that it was going to be on the number-one network had something to do with it. . . . It's a whole new door into the world of television that's opened for me, and now I won this award [the Golden Globe] already, so I feel pretty secure. I have a lot of respect for this type of show."

Sci-Fi

The time-travel aspect as well as all of the rules that accompany it seem daunting, and *QL* has been dismissed too easily as "just sci-fi," which is not the case. Although all of the cast and crew seem to enjoy the science-fiction elements, there is something beyond that, some larger issue.

No one believes this more strongly than Bellisario. "The show's premise is science fiction, but the premise is not what the show's about," he explains. "It's true that we focus on a man traveling through time, but the main focus is on this character who just turns up in places without a memory of why he's there and has to deal with things, like flying a plane, that he has no knowledge of. It's a condition I think viewers can relate to.

"If you're only looking at the premise, then *Quantum Leap* is a science-fiction show. But I believe once you get beyond that premise, you see what we have is what I initially intended: a dramatic anthology which focuses on character and story rather than science fiction."

Creativity Unleashed

With its basic promise established, the series went into production and began slowly to build a following. "Those first thirteen episodes were very hard work," Bellisario recalls. "It's not easy doing anything you want. We had to set down many rules. Everything in this show is period, and period can get awfully expensive.

"Execution to this point has been the hard part. Sitting down to write a script and thinking, 'Well, can we do this on three standing sets and with only two actors?' We don't have the money to do time travel right, so we've had to be creative to be able to do this show as well as we have."

Play it Again, Scott

This creativity has helped bring out the best the show has to offer. Scott Bakula, for one, really appreciates the effort the writers have given to Sam's character. "They keep writing Sam in a way I really like," he says. "I like his values and I like his relationships with people around him. I'm a real people person. One of the reasons I got into this business was that I really like working with people. I can't sit at a computer on a desk all day and be fulfilled. The whole series is me getting into other people's lives and relating with the people in that person's life. I like that a lot."

He continues, "There *is* a lot of me in Sam. Don wrote a character that attracted me to it and attracted him to me. So, I fit in many ways. Originally, I think he pictured Sam to be a little bit more outrageous than I've played him to be. But Don has told me that he's very happy with how I am playing this guy.

"We are at a place right now where the writers may be thinking of a story or just an idea. If they want input, they come to me or Dean and they talk to us. I helped a lot on the 'La Mancha' show. I've done a lot of theater. Paul Brown, who wrote it, came to me and we just talked summer-stock stories for a while. I have ideas for the show, certainly, but so does everybody in the world."

Playing Al

Dean Stockwell has his own ideas about the series and his character, Al. He says, "There was the concern of whether I would continue to play the character over an extended period of time and not have him become repetitious and boring. I also had the normal, human fear of whether or not I would have a costar I could get along with. Given the fact that Scott is the only person I have scenes with in this show, it would've been hell if we didn't hit it off. But I got very lucky because Scott is a joy to work with.

"I'm *not* playing myself," Stockwell continues. "I've always worked through intuition in creating my characters and that's the way it is with Al. I'm quite a bit different from this character. He's much more flamboyant and flippant than I am. A guy like Al looks at environmental problems and political and social situations in a humorous way, while I tend to take them very seriously.

"He's conscious of the negative things going on in the world, but they don't disturb him very deeply. Al just plain enjoys life in a different way than I do, but it's a way of life that I've instilled in him."

A Lone Ranger

As Bakula observes, everyone has ideas for the show; no one more so than creator Don Bellisario. "According to the way Don has set it up," Bakula says, "Sam may be being used as an instrument of healing or humanity or justice or whatever you want to call it. I think Don coined it last year, that Sam's a Lone Ranger type of guy who gets in there, works out problems, and gets out. I'm not sure, but the intention seems to be that by Sam learning, he will then get back to the present. Sam learns every week, and, hopefully, the viewer learns through Sam.

"Again, it's not something Don is trying to beat people over the head with. Subliminally, Sam learns when he is a black man, when he's a woman, when he's mentally retarded. He's constantly being exposed to things."

Bakula concludes, "He's becoming kind of—if it's possible—used to leaping in and out of bodies. One of the things that attracted me from the beginning is that Don thinks of great stories and he always puts a twist in them. So, very seldom am I sitting there while reading a script, saying, 'Oh, I know how this is going to end.' I've learned now that I never know how it's going to end, and that goes for the show as a whole."

4

Leap Speak

The cast and crew of *Quantum Leap* have made several appearances over the last few years to help explain the complexities of the show to confused neophytes and to celebrate with the fans. What follows was just such a conversation held at the University of California at Los Angeles, on Monday, November 26, 1990. Stars Scott Bakula and Dean Stockwell, creator Don Bellisario, co-executive producer Deborah Pratt, and producer Michael Zinberg all attended. The panel answered a series of revealing questions, and the fans were obviously excited and enthused.

Q: I read an interview, I think it was in the *Times*, with Mr. Bakula, and he said that he'd like to play a character with AIDS. Is there anything that's off limits, that you won't touch?

Bakula: I don't think a show like ours need be bound by too many things you can or cannot do. It's unfortunate there is even an AIDS show to do, but we might be able to do a different one than the other shows and shed some different light on it.

Bellisario: It's a tough one. We do not have an AIDS show in the works, although I don't feel that there's anything off-limits for *Quantum Leap*. We have been working on a show where Sam leaps in as a gay. That has *not* worked out to date. It's been written by . . . we've had a gay writer working on it. I'm not happy with the script. It's a tough subject.

I want to present it in a balanced light. I want to be able to represent all views. I hate bigotry, be it against gays, blacks, minorities of any kind.

(*The episode in which Sam leaps into a homosexual was finally produced in the third season.*)

Pratt: We got a pitch about a twelve-year-old boy, and the story deals with his family's acceptance of his fate. It's so heavy, it's a matter of finding the heart and the warmth and the humor.

Bellisario: The show is a very difficult show to write. It looks easy; it's not. It's a very tough show to write, with all the parameters we've set up for it. So, yes, there's nothing off-limits. I've never had the network say to us, "You can't do this, or we don't want you to do this."

Q: Is there anywhere people can write and get a glossy . . . ?

Stockwell: 100 Universal City Plaza, Universal City, California 91608.

Q: (For Deborah Pratt) It's very unusual to find a woman in the position you have. I was wondering whether you were planning a show on abortion.

Pratt: A lot of it comes from my past. Summers in the South. Summers in California, 1965 (*laughs slightly*). Just experiences. Life experiences and trying to understand them and help people to understand what goes on. The unique, wonderful thing about taking Sam Beckett and putting him into someone's life is that all of a sudden you have these fresh eyes looking on a perspective from the middle out. I get to say a lot of things that I believe, that I question, and—so far it's worked out pretty good. I'm writing a show now where he comes back as a sixteen-year-old pregnant woman, eight and a half months pregnant.

Q: (For Scott Bakula) Are you planning to pursue a singing career?

Bakula: I'd love to go back to Broadway sometime. I sing as often as I can. Before I came out here, I spent ten years in New York, doing predominantly musical theater, and I had a rock band from the fourth grade on, so I've been singing a lot. They're very good about letting me do it on the show, and they work it in very nicely, in a lot of different ways. So I'm real lucky that way.

Q: (For Scott Bakula) Can you tell me what your favorite episode was, and why?

Bakula: That's hard for me. There are aspects of every episode, almost, that I enjoy, because every episode is different. I really loved the first episode this year, going back home. That ranks as one of my favorites. I love the episode where I played a young retarded man. I love the "La Mancha" episode that Don directed. I loved the Watts show. I loved the episode where I played a lawyer in the Deep South, I love the episode where . . . it goes on and on. I'm the luckiest guy in town, to play this show.

Bellisario: You saw him playing his father in that episode, which was a terrific job.

Stockwell: Was that him?

Bellisario: That was him.

Q: I missed the first pilot movie, and I was wondering if there were any plans to rebroadcast that movie.

Bellisario: Not at this time they don't. They did rebroadcast it once, the second year.

Stockwell: I betcha there's someone here that might have it.

Pratt: *Quantum Leap* is the second-most-taped show on television.

Bellisario: That's because we're on Friday night at eight. People are not watching television. We're trying to move back. We've been trying. Our audience is definitely not a Friday-night audience. We have a pretty hip audience, and those people aren't hanging around watching television on Friday night.

Q: Where did you get the idea for the series?

Bellisario: It, uh . . . where do you get an idea? No, I won't go into that.

Pratt: Four o'clock, one morning . . .

Bellisario: She can tell you that. We happen to be married, so . . .

Pratt: Four o'clock one morning, he goes, "Hey, hey, hey! Listen to this! Okay. There's this guy, he travels around in time. But he only travels within his own life-time, so he doesn't go back, 'cause that's not believable. . . . " As if traveling in time is believable?

"And he's got a sidekick who only he can see."

I said, "Yeah, but when he goes in, doesn't he . . . "

He says, "No, no, no. He goes in and people see him kinda. . . . "

And I'm going, "Wait, it's four o'clock in the morning. At least let me get a cup of coffee and wait here!"

Bellisario: It's true.

Actually, what happened was, I wanted to create a series that was different, and I wanted to be able to do an anthology. Television networks and studios don't want to do anthologies, because people really don't watch them and they're very hard to syndicate so that they can recover their money; they deficit-finance these things. And I just wanted to do something that would have a different story to tell every week. And I thought, "How can I do it?"

I was reading *Coming of Age in the Milky Way*. I was reading Einstein's theory of time, and I suddenly went, "Wait a minute, what if I did a time-travel show? No way, nobody believes a time-travel show."

Like Deborah said, I woke up at four one morning

and said, "What if he only travels in his own lifetime? People will believe *that*. And if I can get a star or two that people will like to watch every week, they'll tune in to watch them on their adventure and then I can do any kind of story I want to do every week, and that'll be a lot of freedom."

And, boy, was I wrong on that. It's so hard to write this show, as I say. I was right and I was wrong. That's how it really came about.

Q: This question is directed to the three producers, or maybe to Mr. Bellisario. I know that you write a lot of the episodes yourself, and your wife, and I was wondering whether all the episodes are staff-written, or whether you have some freelance submissions to the show.

Bellisario: No, the episodes are not all staff-written. We take outside submissions if they come through an agent. We look for writers all the time.

It's very difficult to find a writer that can do the show. It doesn't matter how good the writer is, the show is a really tough show to write. You have to know what's really going on and what we're looking for. But, yes, we do have outside writers.

Q: Do you publish a guideline for writers as to the rules?

Bellisario: Yeah, the rules of what you can and cannot do. And then the story arenas that we're looking for, and hopefully people come in with fresh ideas. Usually, what happens is that people come in with the ideas that we've already been exploring, which is what makes it difficult.

Q: Do you have any ideas in the works for Sam jumping into the future?

Pratt: We've had pitches and we've tossed around Sam coming into the future. There's a whole trip that's one stumbling block after another. And one from a production standpoint of view—when you create the future, it's pretty well all new. We have a budget, and we have to adhere to it. We have a very short shooting schedule. So we have not quite come up with a way to do it.

Bellisario: We probably will go into the future at some point.

Stockwell: It's a hard show to write. We've been trying to think of an environmental story, and it's hard to fit it into the *Quantum Leap* equation.

Bellisario: See, we really like to do an upbeat show as much as possible. The one in Watts was probably the most "down" ending we've ever done. I just didn't want to do that kind of show. I wanted to do a show that was fun and uplifting and everybody walked away with a good feeling, and maybe learned a little something in the process. In the future, I wanted to take Dean and have him take us through the waiting room, and the imaging chamber, and all of those things. And that is a big production problem, and it's very costly.

Q: (For Dean Stockwell and Scott Bakula) Do you have any future projects in the works besides *Quantum Leap*?

Bakula: No, not at this time.
Stockwell: No.

Q: (For Don Bellisario and for Scott Bakula) As a person who spends time in the lives of these different people, what is Sam's theory of their experience the moment that Sam leaps out of their lives?

Bellisario: I can tell you where they go while Sam is living their lives. They're in the waiting room, which is a medical-looking room.
Pratt: Very antiseptic.
Bellisario: Very antiseptic, with people in white garments or robes, all enclosed and examining them and probing them and checking them; a lot of strange lights, futuristic. And when they come back and leap back, they immediately think that they have been kidnapped by aliens. And if you check, that's when it all started, y'know, right about the time Sam started leaping. All these encounters of the third kind began to happen. They were all quantum leaps.

There will be a three-parter that will take place in the same town over three decades, in which Sam will leap into three different people. So he will solve some problem in the first decade, the fifties, and there will be an overall story, probably a murder to solve, a three-decade-long murder. And he will leap into one character, leap out, and be in the same town ten years later, and in another character. And then we will meet the first character that he leaped into, who has now come back. So we'll have to address exactly what you asked. And Deborah's addressing that at the moment.

Bakula: Well, y'know, I make up a lot of my own stuff as we go. But this is just in my own, y'know, little mind as I'm doing some of this stuff. There's a part of me that feels—in this make-believe world that I find very real—that deep, deep, deep in this person's body, in their subconscious, that part of that subconscious is aware of what happens. Just as part of my subconscious that's left in the present is aware of what's happening. It doesn't manifest itself while I'm in that body. But when I'm gone, there is a trace, there are traces of what went on.

Bellisario: Jung.

Bakula: The double leap, in the Italian episode. The guy came back and he was like, "Whoa." And the girl-friend said, "You look like you got hit on the head or something, you got a headache." And he said, "I don't remember anything," or whatever.

Pratt: "Talk about your earth moving."

Bakula: Yeah, that's right. So that's, y'know, that's just my own little rationale. So, he or she, they're not coming back totally. . . . Someone says, "Just yesterday, you saved that little boy from drowning and you breathed in his mouth." And there's something that says, "Oh, yeah, did I? I don't . . . " So it's not like total amnesia. But see, that's just me. I made that all up myself.

Bellisario: Works for me.

Pratt: On page seven of the handbook, you always say that when Sam leaps out, he leaves that person's life a better place for when they come back in.

Q: (For Scott Bakula) I would like it if someone could leap into my life. As an actor, how did you feel working against no one, doing the scenes with you and yourself as your father, and then having to play against nothing, and then . . .

Bakula: Yeah. It was very hard. I think when they did *Back to the Future*, the guy who applied my makeup had done all the makeup for *Back to the Future*. He talked about, y'know, "For six months, we worked on this one scene." And we did it all in ten days. I was scared to death about it because I, literally, I was up at two-thirty, and I went into prosthetics at three, and at seven o'clock, everybody came in to start work, and I'd be ready to shoot at around eight o'clock. We'd shoot my father all morning, and then at lunch, I'd take the makeup off and shoot the other side of the scene the rest of the afternoon. It was scary because you don't know how it's gonna come out. I had to trust my director. I had input from everybody else who was watching dailies—Don, Deborah, Michael—(*indicates* Dean) and *this* guy helps me tremendously all the time.

Stockwell: And my mother.

Bakula: And your mother was there, that's right. It was kind of a little bit of a crapshoot. Fortunately, I felt the script was exceptionally well written, and so most of my work in that area was already done. So I just had to hope that I was pulling it off, and you don't always know. I hadn't done this ever before.

Stockwell: He never pulled it off, though, until the end of the day, when the work was done. I mean the prosthetics.

Bellisario: Scott always goes into every character. It's an interesting thing. Doing television you're so rushed. Scott studies the character for the next script that he's gonna play while he's playing another character. So he has to prepare for one character while playing another character, which is extremely difficult. In this case, he had to do, y'know, two of them to prepare for. Then Scott came to us and said, "Gee, I'd like to come in and loop some of those lines 'cause I want to make sure that the dad comes off really the way I'd like to see him come off." I don't think you had, to my knowledge, that much to do, because it all came off. So he hit it in front of the camera. He was consistent in playing his father in the mornings, and then he was consistent in playing himself the rest of the day—according to the character— playing himself at age sixteen, which is very difficult, and I think a tribute to his acting ability.

Bakula: You don't often get a chance to play anything like that anywhere in your career, so, y'know, I felt lucky to even make a stab at it. That was thanks to Don, who said, "You wanna play your father?" NBC fell dead on the floor.

Bellisario: Right. They gave us a little extra money to let you do it, and . . . although we went way over, didn't we, Michael?

Michael Zinberg: Not way over. "Way over" is a relative term.

Q: Who is this person Dean Stockwell's character speaks to all the time and how does he know all this information?.

Stockwell: Ziggy, you mean? Ziggy's not a person.

Bellisario: There's Gooshie. . . .

Stockwell: This was explained, as it were, in the pilot. Ziggy is a name given for a huge computer, a state-of-the-art computer in the present/future tense. He's operated by a guy with bad breath named Gooshie.

I have a handlink to Ziggy which I won't talk about.

Bellisario: He doesn't talk about it because we changed the handlink this year, and he's like a child. Y'know, "I want the old one back."

Stockwell: I want my old handlink back.

Bellisario: "I want the old handlink back. . . . "

Stockwell: Who liked the old handlink?

(*Hands go up, and there are cheers from the audience.*)

Bellisario: Who likes the new handlink?

(*Fewer hands go up.*)

Oh!

Stockwell: All right!

Bellisario: Who knew there was a difference?

Pratt: Ziggy is hooked into every newspaper, every book, every piece of information.

Stockwell: Yeah, Ziggy's a huge computer that can really plug into everything. The explanation in the pilot was that Sam has an implant that was put in his neurons—and what's the other, mesons?

Bakula: Mesons.

Stockwell: His optical . . .

Bellisario: He does not know what he's saying, I'm telling you.

Stockwell: So that he, at a certain frequency, can see this hologram.

Bakula: This is incredible, because I only thought you remembered your own lines.

Stockwell: I change my own lines. So this hologram can go back where Sam is in time and he can see him, and he's the only one who can see him.

Stockwell: Until the Christmas show.

Bakula: The Christmas show.

Bellisario: It *sounds* complex; it's very simple. It simply is that, where Dean is standing is an imaging chamber; it's a vast chamber, miles across, empty, nothing there. When he tunes in, or the computer tunes him in to Sam, everything, Sam and everything around Sam, appears as a hologram in that chamber. To Sam, Al appears as a hologram. There's nothing else in the chamber. If he touches something—we did that one episode, in the music episode, where he held a music stand.

Pratt: "Blind Faith."

Bellisario: The minute he let go of the music stand, it disappeared. If Al is touching something, Sam can also see that. That's it. It's just a hologram. They're both holograms to each other. One in 1995 . . .

Pratt: 1997, we've been on for two years.

Bellisario: One in whatever year he's in. It's a device.

Stockwell: You said it's a big room. I like that. Miles, huh?

Q: Will Sam ever get that great beard that his character had at the end of "Sibling Rivalry"?

Bakula: That would make it hard for the woman roles, unless we do another circus show.

Stockwell: I loaned him my beard. It was just for the one movie.

Q: It seems Sam has been a little cranky compared to past seasons. He doesn't hear Al out sometimes; he seems to want to get in and get out as soon as possible, and then he gets involved and gets to care about them. He always gets to love these people by the time he leaves them. I was wondering if that was intentional.

Bellisario: We don't write 'em that way. This is a personal thing going on. There's nothing intentional, really. I'll have to look at that.

Pratt: In any good script, you look for conflict. Sometimes that works as conflict. If it's in there, it's just to give Dean something different to play, or give Scott something different to play, so that we can give them different attitudes about different situations. It's good scriptwriting.

Bakula: I've . . . had my period?

Q: I have a question for the writers. Why do you seem so unwilling to go into a different century?

Bellisario: Ah! It's going to sound crazy, but I truly believe that if you leap him into the Civil War, if you leap him into Rome, it becomes unbelievable. It's believable if he's in the fifties or the sixties, because people have cars, they look a lot alike, they dress the same, they talk the same. It's more believable that way. It's the only thing I can tell you. It's just a personal thing, that's why I did it. I just felt it would be totally unbelievable, everybody would be looking and going, "Oh, yeah, right, he's wearing a Roman toga, yeah, right."

Q: I wasn't born in the fifties, so it's unbelievable for me.

Bellisario: The fifties? Well, see, I'm so old, it's . . .

Q: (For Dean Stockwell) Why are you holding your cigar? It's not lit.

Stockwell: It went out. I can remedy that.

Q: How and why did Sam get chosen to do these leaps?

Bellisario: In the pilot episode, Sam is a quantum physicist who has developed an experiment called "Quantum Leap," a project where he's gonna travel in time. He goes into an accelerator and figures out how do to this. They punch the buttons, and he goes flying off into time, but *somebody* interferes. "Somebody" could be Time, it could be God, it could be Fate, it depends on what you want to believe it is. That person has said, "How dare you go leaping about in time? I'm gonna grab you and I'm gonna use you. I'm gonna use you to do good, and I'm gonna use you to change some things that went wrong."

That's the concept. He's hoping if he can continue to change things, maybe one of these times, whoever's jerking his string will jerk him back to his own time, and he'll then return to where he. . . . In the meantime his attitude is, "I'm gonna enjoy this."

In the very first episode, he got to talk to his father, who was dead, and he said, "This isn't so bad." As Al said at the end of one episode, "I'd give anything to be able to talk to my brother again, my sister, my father, mother, the whole thing."

Q: It's made us all think about our own families.

Pratt: Yeah.

Q: (For Deborah Pratt) As a journalist making the transition to writing, I was wondering how you made the transition from being an actress to a writer and a producer and some of the difficulties you had.

Pratt: I got very angry as an actress, as a black actress, as a female actress, because the roles were so limited. So I locked myself up in my apartment and I started writing, and I·started knocking on doors and using every contact that I have. I had a friend whose father was a producer at Columbia and I said, "Will you please read this?" And it was a late-night soap, 1979. He liked it and he put it into development. It became a daytime soap. It didn't sell, but it made me think, "Oh, wow, I can do this."

I had a background in comedy, so I started writing comedy. Mr. Bellisario hired me as an actress and I had the chutzpahs, or whatever you call it, to come up and say, "I wrote a script for *Airwolf*, and would you read it?" And he says, "So you want to be a writer?" I said, "Yes." And he said, "Well, this is wrong and this is wrong and this is wrong and this is wrong and this is wrong. . . . Rewrite it!"

Bellisario: Page one was okay.

Pratt: So by about my seventh rewrite, it got made, and I enjoy seeing the magic of a script turned into film. One of my favorite things.

Bellisario: Deborah's really good at writing social issues. She likes to deal with those; she does great on writing the stories about women. I think you've written—three now, where he's leaped in as a woman.

Pratt: Just two.

Bellisario: Well, you're writing the third.

Pratt: Oh, three, yeah.

Bellisario: You're writing the third right now, where he leaps in as a pregnant woman, and you've written two where he leaps into a black.

Pratt: I wrote fluff, too. "Sea Bride" was fluff. That was it.

Q: [For Dean Stockwell] I was wondering who designs the clothing that you wear.

Stockwell: Al is a character, and I play the character, and he has a costume and a costume designer. As a matter of fact, when we started this, Don and I had some conversations about it, serious ones, about how the guy would look. We decided that we needed someone to help us come up with the concept of something really off-the-wall. Don knew of this gentleman, Jean-Pierre Dorléac, who was nominated for an Emmy for a show. He should have won, but did not win it, unfortunately. He's the one that puts together all of my outfits. We started out together, and we went shopping. He made some and we got on a frequency where we both knew what it was going to be and we liked it. Now I don't even have to. Whatever he sends down, I put on—ninety-five percent of the time. He's good.

He comes up with great stuff. I pick stuff out myself sometimes, but we understand it and it's consistent, although it's always different. I'm glad you like it. This is no reflection of what I go to work in.

Q: I think a lot of people were nominated for Emmys that should've won.

Bakula: Thank you.

Bellisario: Absolutely. When Scott came in and read, I didn't want to say right on the spot, "Oh, boy, you're the guy!" y'know, and get all excited and then he would go wild and ask for eight million dollars. He came in, he read, he walked out, and it was the first time I'd met Scott. I said, "He's perfect. This is the guy."

Then when I heard Dean would be interested in doing it, I was really excited. Dean had just finished *Married to the Mob*. Dean came in and read and he was the character. He was just there. It was wonderful. It's been that way ever since.

These guys are just great to work with. Nonstar stars. By that, I mean no attitude on either one of them. They're just there to work and have fun. The whole set reflects it. It's just a lot of fun.

Q: (For Dean Stockwell) How difficult was it for you to go from being a child actor to an adult star? It seems like in Hollywood it's very difficult to make that transition.

Stockwell: It was tough, but, I don't think anyone in any field of endeavor has an easy time going from childhood to adulthood. Y'know, it had its difficulties and I'm grateful that I made it through and I'm doing well.

5

Star Biographies

Scott Bakula (Sam Beckett)

As Scott Bakula's Sam "leaps" into a different life each week, the versatile actor spans a wide spectrum of roles that tap his dramatic, comedic, musical, and athletic skills. Bakula received a 1988 Tony nomination for his performance in the musical *Romance, Romance*. Leaping to the big screen for the first time last year, he landed the lead in *Sibling Rivalry*, with Kirstie Alley. In 1991 he starred in *Necessary Roughness*, and in the NBC movie *In the Shadow of a Killer*.

Bakula is a native of St Louis. At thirteen he sang with his church group and the St. Louis Symphony. During high school he divided his time among tennis, soccer, and amateur musical-theater productions. He attended the University of Kansas for one year and then returned to St. Louis to work in community theater.

Bakula moved to New York in 1976, and soon was

cast in *Shenandoah*. His Off-Broadway credits include *Three Guys Naked from the Waist Down*. He made his Broadway debut portraying Joe DiMaggio in *Marilyn: An American Fable* before moving to Los Angeles in 1986 to star on stage in *Nite Club Confidential*.

Dean Stockwell (Al)

Dean Stockwell won a Golden Globe Award (1990) for his portrayal of Al, the lecherous holographic scientist. The role marks the ex–child actor's first continuing character.

A 1989 Oscar nominee and a New York Film Critics Circle Award winner for his performance in *Married to the Mob*, Stockwell also won raves in recent years for his work in the feature films *Blue Velvet*; *Tucker*; *Paris, Texas*; *Beverly Hills Cop* II; and *To Live and Die in L.A.* More recent movies include *Backtrack*, with Dennis Hopper, and *Sandino*, with Kris Kristofferson.

Stockwell's TV credits range from the live drama of *Playhouse 90* and *Hallmark Hall of Fame* to the miniseries *Son of the Morning Star* and guest roles on *Columbo* and *Murder, She Wrote*.

Stockwell made his Broadway debut at age six in *Innocent Voyage* and was signed to an MGM contract. As a child, he starred in eighteen more films, including *The Boy with Green Hair*, *Gentlemen's Agreement*, and *Anchors Aweigh*.

After graduating from high school at sixteen, he left Hollywood and took odd jobs for five years. Upon returning to acting, he starred in the film classics *Compulsion*, *Sons and Lovers*, and *Long Day's Journey Into*

Night before quitting show business a second time. It wasn't until the last decade—after he married and began a family life—that he found himself in demand once again.

Fifty Years of Dean Stockwell: A Career in Brief Television Appearances

Front Row Center "Innocent Witness" (3/4/56)

CBS *Matinee Theater* "Class of '58" (7/9/56)

NBC *Matinee Theater* "Horse Power" (10/30/56)

NBC *Matinee Theater* "Julie" (12/5/56)

NBC *Schlitz Playhouse of Stars* "Washington Incident" (12/7/56)

CBS *Climax* "Murder Is a Witch" (8/15/57)

CBS *Wagon Train* "The Ruth Owens Story" (10/9/57)

NBC *Matinee Theater* "Fight the Whole World" (12/27/57)

NBC *G.E. Theater* "God Is My Judge" (4/20/58)

CBS *Restless Gun* "Mercy Day" (10/6/58)

NBC *Wagon Train* "The Juan Ortegas Story" (10/8/58)

NBC *Cimarron City* "Kid on a Calico Horse" (11/22/58)

NBC *G.E. Theater* "The Family Man" (2/22/59)

CBS *Playhouse 90* "Made in Japan" (3/5/59)

CBS *Wagon Train* "The Rodney Lawrence Story" (6/10/59)

NBC *Johnny Staccato* "The Nature of the Night" (10/15/59)

NBC *The Killers* (11/19/59)

CBS *Checkmate* "The Cyanide Touch" (10/1/60)

CBS *June Allyson Show* "The Dance Man" (10/6/60)

CBS *Outlaws* "Assassin" (2/9/61)

NBC *Alfred Hitchcock Presents* "The Landlady" (2/21/61)

NBC *Wagon Train* "The Will Santee Story" (5/3/61)

NBC *Hallmark Hall of Fame* "The Joke and the Valley" (5/5/61)

NBC *Bus Stop* "Afternoon of a Cowboy" (10/1/61)

ABC *Dick Powell Show* "The Geetas Box" (11/14/61)

NBC *Twilight Zone* "A Quality of Mercy" (12/29/61)

CBS *Alcoa Premiere* "A Place to Hide" (5/22/62)

ABC *Alfred Hitchcock Hour* "Annabel" (11/1/62)

CBS *Dick Powell Show* "In Search of a Son" (11/20/62)

NBC *The Gallant Men* "The Dogs of War" (1/9/63)

ABC *Combat* "High Named Today" (5/7/63)

ABC *Greatest Show on Earth* "The Wrecker" (12/3/63)

ABC *The Defenders* "Climate of Evil" (12/7/63)

CBS *Eleventh Hour* "To Love Is to Live" (4/15/64)

NBC *Kraft Suspense Theater* "Their Own Executioners" (4/23/64)

NBC *Burke's Law* "Who Killed Lenore Wingfield?" (11/4/64)

ABC *Dr. Kildare* "The Bell in the Schoolhouse Tolls for Thee, Kildare" (9/27/65)

NBC *Dr. Kildare* "Life in the Dance Hall: F-U-N" (9/28/65)

NBC *Dr. Kildare* "Some Doors Are Slamming" (10/5/65)

NBC *Dr. Kildare* "Enough *La Bohème* for Everybody" (10/11/65)

NBC *Dr. Kildare* "Now, the Mummy" (10/12/65)

NBC *Dr. Kildare* "A Protechnic Display" (10/18/65)

NBC *Danny Thomas Hour* "The Cage" (1/15/68)

NBC *The* FBI "The Quarry" (10/6/68)

ABC *Bonanza* "The Medal" (10/26/69)

NBC *Mannix* "A Step in Time" (9/27/71)

CBS *The* FBI "Till Death Do Us Part" (10/22/72)

ABC *Columbo* "The Most Crucial Game" (special guest star) (11/5/72)

NBC *Mission: Impossible* "The Pendulum" (2/23/73)

CBS *Streets of San Francisco* "Legion of the Lost" (4/12/73)

ABC *Night Gallery* "Whisper, Whisper" (his brother Guy also guest-starred in this episode) (5/13/73)

NBC *Orson Welles' Great Mysteries* "Unseen Alibi" (11/14/73)

NBC *Police Story* "Collision Course" (11/20/73)

NBC *Police Surgeon* (episode unknown) (5/3/74)

NBC *Police Story* "Love, Mabel" (11/26/74)

NBC *Streets of San Francisco* "The Programming of Charlie Blake" (2/6/75)

ABC *Columbo* "Troubled Waters" (2/9/75)

NBC *Police Story* "The Return of Joe Forrester" (5/6/75)

NBC *Three for the Road* (episode unknown) (11/9/75)

CBS *Cannon* "The Hero" (11/26/75)

CBS *Ellery Queen* "The Adventure of the Blunt Instrument" (12/18/75)

NBC *McCloud* "It Was the Fight Before Christmas" (12/26/76)

NBC *Tales of the Unexpected* "No Way Out" (8/24/77)

NBC *Greatest Heroes of the Bible* "The Story of Daniel in the Lion's Den" (11/22/78)

NBC *Hart to Hart* "Hart's Desire" (11/16/82)

ABC *The A-Team* "A Small and Deadly War" (2/15/83)

NBC *Simon and Simon* "The Skeleton Who Came
     Out of the Closet" (3/31/83)
CBS *Miami Vice* (episodes unknown) (11/22/85,
     2/28/86)
NBC *Murder, She Wrote* "Deadpan" (5/1/88)
CBS *New Twilight Zone* "Room 2426" (1989)
CBS *Quantum Leap* (3/26/89–current)

Stockwell also did the E! Entertainment Channel's
Moments in History segments a year or two back.

Television Movies

Paper Man (11/12/71)
CBS *The Failing of Raymond* (11/27/71)
ABC *The Adventures of Nick Carter* (2/20/72)
ABC *The Return of Joe Forrester* (5/6/75)
NBC *A Killing Affair* (9/21/77) (also listed as an
     episode of the series *Police Story* in some
     sources)
CBS *Born to Be Sold* (11/2/81)
NBC *The Gambler III: The Legend Continues* (11/22/87,
     11/24/87)
CBS *Son of the Morning Star* (miniseries)

Film Performances

Abbott and Costello in Hollywood (1945, MGM)
Alsino and the Condor (Nicaragua) (1983)
Anchors Aweigh (1945, MGM)
Another Day at the Races
Arnelo Affair, The (1947, MGM)

Backtrack (1990)

Banzai Runner (1986)

Beverly Hills Cop II, (1986)

Blue Iguana, The (1988)

Blue Velvet (1986)

Boy with Green Hair, The (1949/50, RKO)

Buying Time (1957)

Careless Years, The (1957)

Catchfire Cattle Drive (1951, Universal-International)

Citizen Soldier (1984)

Compulsion (1959, TCF/Darryl T. Zanuck Productions)

Deep Waters (1948, TCF)

Down to the Sea in Ships (1949, TCF)

Dune (1984)

Dunwich Horror, The (1970, AIP)

Ecstasy (1970)

Gardens of Stone (1987)

Gentlemen's Agreement (1947, TCF)

Green Years, The (1946, MGM)

Gun for a Coward (1956, UI)

Happy Years, The (1950, MGM)

Home, Sweet Homicide (1946, TCF)

Human Highway (actor, cowriter, codirector) (1982)

Kim (1950, MGM)

Last Movie, The (1971, Universal)

Legend of Billie Jean, (1989)

Limit Up, The (1989)

Loners, The (1972, Four Leaf/Fanfare)

Long Day's Journey Iito Night (1962, Ely Landau)

Man with the Deadly Lens, The (1982)

Married to the Mob (1988) (nominated for Academy
    Award: Best Supporting Actor)

Mighty McGurk, The (1946)

One Away (1980)

Palais Royale

Paris, Texas (German/French) (1984)

Psych-Out (1968)

Rapture (1965, International Classics/TCF)

Romance of Rosy Ridge, The (1947, MGM)

Sandino (1990)

Secret Garden, The (1949, MGM)

She Came to the Valley (1979)

Song of the Thin Man (1947)

Sons and Lovers (1960, TCF/Company of Artists/Jerry Wald)

Stars in My Crown (1950, MGM)

Stickfighter Three for the Money (1975)

Time Guardian, The (1987)

To Kill a Stranger

To Live and Die in L.A. (1987)

Tracks (1977)

Tucker: The Man and His Dream (1986)

Valley of Decision, The (1945, MGM)

Werewolf of Washington (1973)

Won Ton Ton, the Dog Who Saved Hollywood (1976, Paramount/David V. Picker, Arnold Schulman, Michael Winner)

Wrong Is Right (1982)

6

More *Leap* Speak

The following is the second in a series of conversations held by the cast and crew of *Quantum Leap* to explain the series and say "Thank you" to viewers. Don Bellisario, Deborah Pratt, Scott Bakula, and Dean Stockwell all appeared. The event took place at Universal Studios, on February 25, 1991, and was transcribed by Sally Smith.

Q: When they're in the waiting room and they come back, do they know what they've been through?

Bellisario: No, they don't know what they've been through. They think that they have been captured by aliens.

Q: (For Dean Stockwell) What are you looking at when you're talking to Sam? Are you looking at Sam, or do you see the person he leaps into?

Stockwell: No, I see the person he leaps into . . . but I know it's him.

Q: (For Dean Stockwell) Who designed your clothes, Al?

Stockwell: Jean-Pierre Dorléac is our costume designer, and he does a great job.

Q: (For Scott Bakula) Will there be further episodes where you'll be showing off your vocal talents?

Bakula: No, they're not letting me sing anymore.
Pratt: That's not true, I wanna bring him back as a Supreme.
Bakula: Actually, there's a big show coming up called "Glitter Rock," where I leap into the lead singer in a very much KISS-like band in the seventies, and there are a couple of original songs in that. And there's also a show called "Piano Man," where I actually was able to write a song for the show and do that, too.

Q: (For Scott Bakula) Were you really eating Jell-O with onions?

Bakula: I was eating Jell-O with—what's it called?—

jicama, thank you! Ten points for the jicama, yeah! It's a hiccup, but it's like a . . .

Stockwell: Gag me with a spoon.

Q: Will any of the first-season shows be re-broadcast?

Bellisario: Well, hopefully because we're moving back to Wednesday night, we'll get renewed for another season. And then following that, I'm sure you'll see the show in syndication, and you'll get to see all those episodes. You may see it in syndication anyway.

Bakula: Or, if you talk to somebody here, I know several people in this room that have all the episodes on tape, so you might be able to work a little exchange.

Q: Up to about five or six episodes into the second season, at the beginning of the show, you did a segue from the previous episode to the current one. Why did that disappear, and will it come back?

Bellisario: As a show goes along, you try to streamline it and to improve it, and initially we were trying to set up all the premises so that everyone would understand what they were. We did what we call a "saga cell"; we still do that to some extent, but it was much more extensive in the beginning, where you came in and we explained the whole concept.

Now we've abbreviated that and just decided that the show would work a little better if we just came into the top of the episode and we didn't have to show what happened the week before. Instead we compressed the time and we did it a little quicker. It was really a matter of saving some time up front.

Q: How did you go about the process of choosing Scott and Dean for their roles, and how do you feel about how your roles have progressed through the years?

Bellisario: The process of choosing was casting, and when Scott came in, and (*to Bakula*) I think you only had sides that first day, didn't you? You didn't have a whole script; he came in and read the sides. I'm sorry. Sides are just scenes; you don't give a whole script out, you just give out one or two scenes, and you have actors come in and read one or two scenes, so they really don't know the whole story of what's going on. It's kinda like a secret project in the works, y'know.

Scott came in and read with a number of other fine actors who came in over a period of about a week or so, and the minute Scott read for that scene I knew he was the guy that should be playing Sam. I waited at least until he walked out of the room before I said that. And Dean . . . when I heard that Dean might be interested in doing it, y'know, I was just ready to kiss his cigar! But they can tell you their second process.

Stockwell: Well, I liked the role and concept and I liked working with Scott right away in the pilot. And what's happened since then is it's continued enjoyment of the role for me. It's getting more and more comfortable, like a really comfortable old friend, this Al.

Bakula: He's the greatest. These things are kinda a whole evolving thing. Don has an idea, and then you put a body into that idea, and then the body has some ideas, and if you're in a good situation—which you're not always—but if you're in a good situation, you combine, and both of you kind of learn from each other and grow together, with Don, Deborah, and all of our other writers. . . Jeff Gourson, in postproduction . . . then everybody kinda just jumps in and adds.

Bellisario: I want to give you one example of how you grow. Deborah can tell you when she wrote one script, Scott took a very risky chance. He chose to really identify with the sixteen-year-old girl, and to get very emotionally involved. That's probably not a choice that initially I ever had in mind. We'll have to ask Deborah if she had that in mind for him to do it that strongly.

(Pratt *says no.*)

That was a choice that Scott made. I think it was an excellent choice, and the character expands because of that, and I think that in another episode that we do we'll keep in mind the choice that Scott made. So you see, it really is a collaborative effort of making the show go.

Q: It seems like I still see *Kim* when I'm watching Al on the screen. Did that movie have any bearing on your choice of him as a character, and whether Al is still playing *Kim*?

Stockwell: You know, that's interesting. I never thought of that before, but now that you mention it, there are elements of that character in Kim. He was a little bit lascivious, he was a very young letch, he smoked a cigar. I guess maybe there's a little bit of Kim in there. That's interesting.

Q: Favorite episodes for everyone?

Pratt: That's a hard question, in the sense that each one means something. I wrote the one that we're shooting now, which is now my favorite one. I mean, whatever one that I write I fall in love with because it's part of me, and I put part of myself and my background and my family and all those things that I was raised to be in it. I don't think you can separate that.

Bellisario: It's a little like asking which of your children is your favorite child, it really is. You love different children for different reasons; they're all different, and I know about that—this is gonna be number seven (as he points to wife, Deborah Pratt). She's trying to make me a rock star. But each child is different, and each show is different, so you really don't have a favorite. I know I don't have a favorite; I can name you a lot of shows that I liked for various reasons.

Bakula: Well, I have basically more of the same. There are elements of every show that become very special to me. I'll be specific and name about four or five, maybe—this year. I loved "The Leap Home"; I loved playing opposite the devil in the Halloween show; I loved "La Mancha"; "Jimmy"; "Seymour"; it just goes on and on . . . "Volare." What a great thing to be able to say that, that there are just so many special episodes. It's a real credit to the writers on the show.

Stockwell: I gotta second that. I don't have a favorite either, except the pilot, because that was the first. . . .

Bakula: The "M.I.A." show was a great show, too.

Q: (For Scott Bakula) Just to elaborate, which was the most challenging for you?

Bakula: For me? That also takes on a whole . . . there are all different elements to that question. Some shows are challenging because physically they're very difficult, some are emotionally very difficult. This was kind of a combination show. Physically, I mean, I was in transition for like sixteen hours. That little last scene from me coming in the doorway at the hospital at the end, I mean we started at eight in the morning and wrapped at, I don't know, eleven o'clock at night. That's a long day to—uh, push. So that was a tough one. So it's hard . . . the show is wonderfully difficult, in many different ways, and challenging.

Q: Are there any plans to leap Sam into animals?

Bakula: The rock-and-roll guy was as close to an animal as . . . I looked a little bit like Ron Perlman. In clown whiteface.

Bellisario: We have thought about leaping Scott into an animal. He'd have to be naked, of course, and Standards and Practices wouldn't like that, so we'll have to deal with that.

Bakula: I could be a poodle with a little suit on!

Q: In the first season, when Scott first leaped into a woman, I thought it was a really great idea, a guy actually having to be in a woman's body and dealing with it, and then having to be in a blind man's body, and so forth. You went a little bit different than what I thought, but that's okay, because you're the executive producer. What I was wondering was whether it would be more challenging to Sam as a person if he instead of just having the difficulty of being perceived as a woman, actually had to deal with the physical limitations of being a woman?

Bellisario: The women that I talk to tell me they don't have any physical limitations.

No, I don't think so, and I'll tell you why. A lot of what we do on the show is about people are perceived . . . If he had leaped into Jimmy and truly been a person who had a handicap or was retarded, then I don't know what we'd've been accomplishing with that. Sam might have learned something out of it, but he learns something leaping in and being himself and being perceived as being a retarded person. That means that people see you as something, they treat you like it, and they don't give you a chance to be who you could be.

That's part of what we're talking about, part of what we're trying to change. So the idea is not that he really is that person. That never was the concept. The concept in my head was that when he leaped in, people saw the aura of the person he leaped into. It's a little bit like if I came up here at the beginning of this thing as I did, and I somehow hypnotized you all and instead of Scott Bakula being up here, because he was down working on the show, I had Michael Zinberg—who's a producer—come up and sit down here, and you all saw him as Scott Bakula. That's what happens on the show.

It's only when you look in a mirror do you see, do we see, does Scott see, what everybody sees around him. I think that holds true. And I think that's also interesting, because he can leap in as a very old man that everyone can perceive cannot do anything and he can be quite physical and shock people when that happens. Or he can leap in as a man his age—he's not very old, but he can be trying to perform as a boxer who's twenty years old. Tough to do. He is then handicapped in that situation, by his limits.

Q: (For Dean Stockwell and Scott Bakula) What'll you do during hiatus?

Stockwell: I don't know. We have three more shows to shoot now, then we're off for a couple months, and I'm trying to get a feature. I hope to get one or two things. Other than that, it's nine months of *Quantum Leap*.

Bakula: There are a couple of things that may or may not happen. Oddly, I'm overwhelmed right now with the sense of starting over after three years generating an audience again for the show, which starts in two weeks. I'm a little overwhelmed by that, so the things maybe down the line right now are not really in great focus. This is the focus, and thanks to you all, I think we have a really good shot at it.

Q: Does Sam have recollections of his previous encounters when he enters into a new guy?

Bakula: Yeah, I think we don't deal with this very often anymore because so many of the viewers know the rules now that we don't go back into the Swiss-cheese thing. We mention it periodically, and I make the mistakes still. I think there's a little Swiss-cheesing that happens all the time. I think I remember certain things; I don't think we've ever done this really, except in one show where I deal with this in the middle of the show in the very beginning, the Italian episode, the hit-man episode.

We've never leaped from one show and brought him into another and had him dealing with that last memory exactly. I think the other thing that would be a problem if we carried over is that down the line from now, if shows are played in a different order, it would really kind of screw them up. It makes each show kind of a little total.

Bellisario: What Scott's making reference to is that down the line in reruns, be it on the network or in syndication, you could chop off the leap of one show and put the leap of another one on it, and run 'em in a different order, and have him leap in different orders.

Bakula: If I came in and was talking about "Did I have the baby?" you know, that would be hard . . . I think I remember almost everything, though. I think if I leap back into this same year and work on an oil rig, or into that young kid's body, I would remember having been there. Hopefully, next year, we'll do a story like that.

Q: (For Scott Bakula) Your wife, Krista, is an actress. Has she shown any desire to do an episode? Also

have you thought about doing *Love Letters* on hiatus, and when's that album coming out?

Bakula: Krista may do something on the show at some point, but she really is happily hiatusing from the business, and doesn't really miss it. I've been approached a couple of times to do *Love Letters*, but it hasn't ever really worked out, and it may or may not happen sometime. Deborah can give you all the information on the album, 'cause I'm dying to hear about it, too!

Pratt: We're working very hard to take all the music from the show, all the songs that Scott's done, and put them on an album. We're in negotiations—in talks, I won't even say negotiations—with MCA right now to put out all the songs.

Q: Do you accept unsolicited story ideas?

Bellisario: We can't do that. I'm sorry about that, we really can't, and the reason is very simple: We get sued a lot. It's difficult, and I know there are a lot of people who are young and want to do it. The only way you can ever submit something like that is to sign a form which literally signs all your rights away, which says that if we ever use anything from yours, you can't sue us for it or claim for it. It's a terrible form, but it's the only way we can protect ourselves because we're working on stories all the time.

I would say that writers who come in who are professional writers in the business, who have been sent in by agents to pitch us stories, I'd say eighty percent of the stories that they pitch us we've already considered. What happens when you have writers on the outside coming up with story ideas is that when they then see an idea that they've pitched—it may have been in the works a year ago or six months ago—they think, "Oh, you ripped me off, and I'm gonna sue you." I'm not saying you would do that, but I've been through enough lawsuits that we can't do it. If you wanna contact my office and then accept the form which Harriet Margulies will send and fill that form out, and sign your life away to Universal Studios, then you can do it. By the way, before I forget, I do wanna thank Harriet, who put this all together.

Q: (For Scott Bakula) After *Quantum Leap* is over in about five or ten years, is there a definitive role that you've never played that you'd like to play?

Bakula: I've been really lucky in the last few years in the theater to create new things. There's some wonderful roles that I'd like to do. I'd like to do *La Mancha* again, I did it when I was twenty-one. I'm really into the creative process from day one. I don't know; I would like to do *Sweeney Todd* sometime, that's one of my favorite shows.

Q: Why haven't the *Quantum Leap* novels been released?

Bellisario: I didn't know that there were three novels released. Are they novels that are released through

Universal? They've got my name on them? Well, that's another one I don't know about!

Stockwell: Ask your accountant!

Bellisario: I don't get paid for that one.

Q: Are you ever gonna do any episodes in the future where Al is?

Bakula: I hope so. If we go on long enough, and Universal will consent to pay the money to do futuristic stuff, I think we can talk this guy into doing it.

Bellisario: I'd like to do it. The last episode, the leap-out? I can give you a little hint, if you all keep it under control for a second.

We're thinking at the end of the last episode, when Scott leaps out, that there's a thunderstorm, and Dean decides that he's getting out of there. Dean goes to walk through a wall and bounces off of it; Scott walks through the wall.

The only problem is that Dean has the control in his hand, so Scott can't leap. Somehow they have switched identities. We haven't worked that out. We're thinking of doing an episode like that.

Q: Are you planning a finishing episode?

Bellisario: Oh, we haven't even thought about that; it's like planning your own death.

7

Creating an Episode

Producers Chris Ruppenthal, Deborah Pratt, and Tommy Thompson, writer Beverly Bridges, art director Cameron Birnie, and consultant Rich Whiteside attended a panel to discuss the creative process behind the series. It took place at Universal Hilton on March 1, 1992.

Q: How do you create ideas?

Pratt: The genesis of ideas?

Ruppenthal: . . . And just how the whole process gets rolling.

Pratt: It's true. Everything starts from the idea. We're very lucky on our staff as writers to have very, very creative people. As a staff writer, you pretty much come up with an idea in what's called an "arena." Sam leaps into an exciting situation, and then the story begins. The hard part is, then the story begins. If you came in kind of out of the blue and pitched to us as what's called a freelance writer, we would find an arena that we like, and a leap-in that we like, and you would sit down with our writing staff and we would begin to talk about the story, and how it works, and who the characters are, the most important being the "heart story" and the relationship with Sam and Al and how Sam drives the story. We have a book, called the bible.

Ruppenthal: Yeah. It's really thick. *Too* thick. About fifty pages of stuff on *Quantum Leap*.

Pratt: There are rules you have to adhere to. It's what's called a layered show. Because Sam and Al leap into this entire new situation every week, and we introduce all new characters every week, we have to have guidelines to how much of Sam comes through the character, how it evolves in the course of the show in what's called the arc, and because it's historical . . . Remember those wonderful kisses with history we used to try to do? They're *very* hard to do, 'cause there's a big rule. Kisses with history have to be immediately recognizable, they have to be funny, they have to come out of left field and kiss the story, and then you move on. They're very tough to do.

Ruppenthal: Not only that, but if that person is still living, you oftentimes have to get their permission. We tried to do one with Madonna; we had to, y'know, approach her agent; it was a great kiss with history, but she turned us down. On the other hand, Stephen King said yes, that's fine. So you never know.

Thompson: Some people we never even ask, though. In the wrestling show we did—was it the wrestling, yeah? No, it was the priest show, we did Sylvester Stallone. We figured if he was bothered by that . . . he must have bigger things to worry about.

Pratt: You want to just talk about a couple of the other rules?

Ruppenthal: Yeah.

Thompson: Chris knows the rules.

Ruppenthal: Tommy doesn't know the rules, that's why his scripts are much better than mine. One thing you should know is that it's never easy for us to come up with an idea, even within our own arenas, sitting around pitching. We sit around for hours banging our heads against the walls, pitching ideas for stories. There are no automatic approvals. The best thing is you get an idea, and you say, "Sam leaps in as a midget-race-car driver." And you go, "That's a great idea! Like, 'Oh, boy!' and he goes out of control." We do the whole story, you work it out, and we write outlines and treatments. Then somewhere down the line—you can almost count on this, which makes it a much better script—someone goes, "Well, what if he was a woman driver?" and it changes. That's the golden monkey wrench. That's a phrase we use around the office.

Thompson: It's usually you.

Ruppenthal: Yeah.

Thompson: You've got this thing all worked out, you're ready to go write it, and Chris'll walk in and go, "What if he's this?" and it's gone. The whole thing is gone.

Ruppenthal: We try to get past that moment anyway. It makes it better. Like in the way, when we did the Halloween episode.

Ruppenthal: We were all sitting around and Tommy

was one of the people who said, "Well—what if Al's the devil?" and he totally causes me to rewrite this entire outline. One of the things you have to remember, and that we always beat on people from the outside writers to ourselves, and we always hear constantly, is that Sam has to drive the story. That's an internal rule that we always go through, whether we think he is pushing the action and advancing plots and overcoming things. It's way too easy—it's a mistake we make ourselves, often—if he just reacts and for three acts stands around and goes, "Oh, cool, oh, wow, why am I here?" So the toughest thing to do is to have him come in and to advance each act, advance each plot beat per se, occasionally with the help of others. Then, once you write this fabulous script, we have to pass it . . .

Pratt: Go back one more step. We are a time-travel show, there's a great deal of research that goes into the period, the look of what we want to set up as writers. You have to set—we write little movies each week, and we really look at it that way, and we have to set the scene and the characters so that people don't use credit cards in 1953, or they don't do things in 1953 that would be something that you would have in 1985, like a car phone.

Thompson: It varies, though, from writer to writer, how much research gets done. I do very little research. Paul Brown flies to other *countries* to research things. He literally flew to Washington, at his own expense, for the chimp show and the show about the deaf girl. I wrote one about a wrestler and all I did was put a picture of a wrestler on my wall. I was writing it and I would look at it occasionally and Paul would come in and go, "This is your research?!" And I'd go, "Yeah!" It just reminds me what I'm writing, it's a wrestler. Chris does a lot of research, everybody does a lot of research—except me.

Pratt: One of the people we call, which is why Rich Whiteside is here, is Rich, because when Don was writing "MIA" and Sam leaped into a navy SEAL, he wanted some authentic stuff, the real stuff.

Whiteside: Well, I had the luxury of time. When Don was preparing to do the Vietnam episode, the two-parter, "The Leap Back," he had about four months before they were actually going in to shoot that, which is probably unusual. He had contacted me, given me the thumbnail sketch of what the show was going to be about and asked me to provide him background information. Unfortunately, he didn't know what he was asking for, 'cause I flooded him with stuff for about four months.

I gave him pictures from guys on the teams in Vietnam. I didn't serve in Vietnam, so I traveled down to Virginia and interviewed guys who were commanders in Vietnam, who did POW repatriation missions, and brought that information back to him. At that time there was a SEAL Team Two twenty-year picture album that came out, so I sent that back to him. I got books that were written by members who served there that detailed missions, highlighted what it was like to be in a firefight from the recipients' standpoint. What was it like to be on a POW repatriation mission? What were the different basic character types that exist in the teams?

Coming from an acting standpoint, I kinda knew what he was looking for, and I tried to feed him things he could digest and put into the story, which also included locations, such as—in SEAL teams in

Vietnam, their activities centered around the bar in camp, their missions, and the bar in town. You saw where the story kind of evolved out of. So he took, on top of that, he layered the story.

I have to give Don and everybody on the staff a lot of credit, because they took the time under an incredibly busy schedule to sit back and listen to what I had to say, and then they incorporated it. That was from costumes, to props, to makeup, all the way down the line. When we were shooting it, Michael Zinberg, who was directing it, before each scene, would call me up and he would say, "This is the way I see the scene developing." I would tell him where there were inconsistencies, just from a military standpoint. If he could make a correction and use it, then he did. If we could come to a compromise, he did. When it came down to artistic license, he made the decision. So that's what it was from my technical standpoint on that one episode.

Pratt: Okay, now Chris is gonna talk a little bit about after the script is done. . . .

Ruppenthal: Yeah. After the script is done, and we turn it in to everyone else, we all get notes. In television, it's a lot more than just writing the first draft. It's the rewriting of it, and rewriting and rewriting and rewriting. All the way through production, quite often. Unfortunately, that will have the impact on two people here also that—Cameron Birnie will tell you, who's our art director, set designer par excellence, and Joe Napolitano, our director is—they tear their hairs out as at the last second you suddenly say, "Well, this scene no longer takes place in an alley, it's in a ballroom for twelve hundred people." It sort of changes your life.

Thompson: It's usually the other way, though.

Ruppenthal: Right. As Tommy said, it usually goes the other way. Usually, we start very big and go small, which is the role of actual money in the production here. It costs a lot of money to do these shows. I think that our postproduction and our production staff do an incredible job of putting every cent on the screen. It's very cheap to write and sit in an office, but what they do every week is fantastic.

Birnie: I guess the first thing that we do is make a set list. When we start to plan the show, we'll start to discuss what locations we're gonna look for that are gonna be practical, and which locations we wanna make.

I remember on one show that we did for Joe, we did "Pool Hall Blues," and that took place almost entirely inside that one set. Because we didn't want the company to move off the stages, there were alley scenes. The most logical time to do an alley is to go out to the back lot out there and shoot New York Street, but sometimes the company is so expensive to move that we built the alley right on the stage. We have problems like that all the time, where sometimes you have to build things you don't expect to build. This show that Joe and I are prepping right now takes place in an Egyptian tomb. There's only two major sets on that show. We're gonna build the tomb, both tombs, on stage, because there's a lot of effects that take place in 'em—mummies and things like that.

Egypt is another one of our problems. Just like in the Vietnam show, sometimes we have to find locations that are almost impossible to find. We have something in the studio called the "thirty-mile zone." That means that we're allowed to find any location we can shoot within thirty miles, 'cause that's as far as we can ship the company. Within thirty miles of Los Angeles, we couldn't find Vietnam. We thought about making Vietnam; we think of all kinds of crazy ideas. We thought we could plant a jungle and make a jungle in a couple days. We finally ended up going outside of the zone to the only place at all that looked like Vietnam, and it did look quite authentically like Vietnam, which was out in the town of Norco, and we were lucky about that. This time we're looking for Egypt.

I don't know where you go to find Egypt in the middle of a drought in Southern California. Then it goes and rains, so every time we had a dry spot, now there's green weeds growing up everywhere. We're lucky enough to find a quarry this time. We found a quarry and we're gonna shoot in this quarry. Unfortunately, it wasn't exactly level. We had about six bulldozers moving a room full of dirt out of the way over the weekend. It actually happened yesterday.

Napolitano: Just part of the fun. Sort of like when you're a child and you play in the sandbox. Except this is a *very* large sandbox.

Birnie: You notice that the directors say "that's part of the fun. I like that part." That's part of the fun for the writers, too.

I was amazed. We're standing on the location up there, and Joe says, "This place is perfect, but I want to be standing where they are down there, eighteen feet below us." Everyone in our group just said, like we usually say, "Okay . . ."

Napolitano: It's all part of telling the story. It's whatever is gonna make it work, that's what's important. That's why the wonderful production staff and the people who support everything that we do . . . we just sit there and we get our ideas and we have our whims. . . . There's a myriad of people who support us to help make this. Yeah, I think we perform magic. We have seven days of preparation and then we shoot the show in eight days. That's basically the way it goes each episode; "Boogieman" was done in seven. We shot it in seven days.

Thompson: Except at the end of the year, when we're out of money.

Ruppenthal: Right.

Napolitano: Yeah.

Thompson: Then you do it in seven days.

Napolitano: I also wanna go public here with one thing. Chris Ruppenthal, who wrote "Boogieman," his nickname since then has been "Ruppenboogie." We needed to go public with that.

Pratt: In that prep time, some of the things that happen are the casting, set design, and any type of props that are needed. We had to look at camels and scorpions because we're in the desert and that's what we're dealing with. Jean-Pierre Dorléac, who will be out in a little bit, designs all the wardrobes. We decide on lighting, any kind of special effects that we need, any type of cars that we need. It's a lot of people doing a lot of things to make this show work. Then we start shooting.

Ruppenthal: It's amazing. They will, at the last second, say, "Y'know, I need a 1957 gas lantern for this episode," and George Tuers goes, "Okay, I'll run out and get one." There are about a hundred people involved in the crew who make this happen. They are around. It is a miracle every week that it gets done, the episode gets done in eight days.

Thompson: The scariest thing is when you say to George, "We need a leather bra with big studs on it," and he gets it, right there in his car. He gets it out of the backseat of his car.

Ruppenthal: He's always terrifying.

Thompson: I don't know what he's got in his trunk, but whatever you need, he's got it in his trunk.

Pratt: Editing happens after that, and then postproduction, where we put in sound effects and visual effects. It's a lot of work, and there's a whole postproduction team that works very, very, very hard. . . . Julie and David Bellisario . . .

Ruppenthal: Jimmy Giritlian, Jeff Gourson, and two of our editors . . . Jon Koslowsky, Michael Stern, who've been doing a great job. And all their assistants.

Pratt: They do what's called the music and effects, where we talk about where we want special effects, lightning and thunder, and where we want music cues to come in, and Ray Bunch comes in and scores for us. Then Julie and the troops put it together and that's how we get it to you.

Q: Who took Sam's clothes off?

Bridges: Ladies, I'm the woman you thank for taking Sam's clothes off. Is that right?

Pratt: Yeah, y'know, it was really funny, 'cause she wrote the script. . . .

Bridges: Oh, "The Play's the Thing." Sam does a nude *Hamlet*.

Thompson: You take 'em off in every episode!

Bridges: Oh, the bounty hunter . . .

Pratt: The first time we did it actually goes back to "Her Charm." I said to him, "Women out there love you with your chest exposed." He said, "No, no, no, no way." I said, "Do me a favor. . . . " "Her Charm," that's right, that's what it was and then you proved it again in . . .

Ruppenthal: "A-Hunting We Will Go."

Pratt: That's the other one. I said, "If the ratings go up because you're out without a shirt, never ever hassle me about it again." Sure enough, we came up three share points.

Ruppenthal: So, thank Beverly for that.

Bridges: It's funny, because originally when I wrote "A-Hunting We Will Go," where Sam's a bounty hunter, in the third act, he has a bedroom scene where his shirt is off. As a writer, I just didn't put it back on for the whole fourth act.

Deborah and I were sitting in a production meeting. In the production meeting, the costume people were there, everybody who has anything to do with production was there. We're the only two women in the room. All the guys said, "Wait a moment. He doesn't have his shirt back on in the fourth act." And Deborah and I go, "Yeah."

"Y'know, it's really cold up there in the Sierra highlands. . . . " So we were overruled by a group full of very modest men, who put the shirt back on. I tried! I tried!

Pratt: We had the opportunity in the deaf show for him to take *all* of his clothes off, so it really makes up for it. When he was the Chippendale dancer.

Ruppenthal: Right. Then we did *Hamlet* naked.

Pratt: You've done it a couple of times, that's right.

Ruppenthal: There's no stopping this woman.

Bridges: It's funny, I met a fan this week and my very

first script that I wrote was "The Great Spontini," and handcuffs played a big part in "The Great Spontini." My second script was "A-Hunting We Will Go," and in most of it, he's handcuffed. Somebody wrote me asking if I was really into bondage.

Thompson: Is there a script that you've written that you haven't mentioned by name yet?

Bridges: "Raped."

Q: In the episode where Sam leaped into a gay college cadet, what was altered in the original script? And what made the advertisers pull out?

Thompson: I did one of the rewrites on that script. It was written by Bobby Duncan, who is a freelance writer. The problem NBC had with it, the big problem, was it was a teenage-suicide story. It was set in a prep school; it was a much younger kid, and he was going to kill himself. That was their biggest problem.

I did a rewrite. I sort of did more of the attitude of Sam defending him and Al having a problem with it, being from an old school.

We aged 'em a little bit, we made the kids older, and it seemed to calm them down a lot. It was funny, I couldn't understand the controversy on the script. I just kept reading and hearing things about it, and these people I don't think had ever seen the script or heard about it. It offended me. I've been disabled since I was fifteen, and I don't lump myself in with every disabled— y'know what I mean? I mean, every story about a disabled person is not about me. I didn't see how that story was so universal and indicted everybody on the planet with this one story line. So it really bothered me, a lot. I don't know what the products were, to tell you the truth.

Ruppenthal: When you deal with a division of Standards and Practices, it's basically a censorship-type deal. They have done studies, the networks, that whenever teenage suicide is portrayed, even if you go through the entire episode saying, "It's bad, don't do it, kids, there's another way out," there is a rise in attempted and successful teenage suicides. So we were only too happy to not contribute to that by making it a college-age situation, where we made a specific point of saying, "I'm twenty-one, I'm old enough to make up my own mind," to make them older. The other point they wanted to do was not to have the gay character seem flagrantly, stereotypically caricatured as a gay person.

Pratt: It never was.

Ruppenthal: It never was. Our whole point was "What's the difference? What's the point?"

Thompson: The last line in the script, the last scene that I wrote, was Al saying, "I still can't remember, I can't figure it out, was he gay?" and Sam says, "Does it matter?" That was the point of the whole script. I don't think that the people that were arguing about it got to that point in the script before they went nuts, y'know what I mean? So, hey, y'know, people have problems with things like that, so you have to deal with them. So that's why you write wrestling shows, where nobody cares.

Q: Has Dean or Scott ever said they won't do something that you've written?

Ruppenthal: Has Dean or Scott ever said they won't do anything?

Napolitano: Yes.

Pratt: They are the darlings of television. They are the best people to work with and for. They each give two hundred percent every time, but there are things that even they . . .

Thompson: They've gotten angry about things before. Not angry, but, um . . . I remember in the beauty-pageant show, I walked down and I saw Scott in that bathing suit with the high heels. He just looked at me and he goes, "I don't know where or when, but I'll get you for this." He hasn't gotten me yet.

Q: Are there any scenes that you've loved but have been cut, either a produced scene or a written scene?

Napolitano: Not really whole scenes. Sometimes as a director, you fall in love with certain shots within a scene, a piece of the scene, and the producers take it out. They usually have good reasons and you just go along with that. It's all for the better, I mean, we're not trying to ruin the show.

Sometimes it's hard to let go of something. Writers have the same problem, I'm sure. They'll write a scene and, in the final edit, maybe only half of that scene will be in there and you'll lose some stuff—but you've gotta do that because sometimes some things get in the way of telling the story. We all just kind of live through it, but it's okay. I'm not complaining. I'm just saying it has to go sometimes.

Pratt: By the time a show gets shot, from a writer's point of view, it pretty much is what it is. There was a scene in "Shock Theater," a conversation between Verbena Beeks and Sam. We ended up losing the audio, because of Ziggy, what Ziggy could and couldn't do. The original ending of "So Help Me God" was a very different ending and, for a variety of reasons, it was changed. So, yeah, there are scenes that change. I think in the long run—and you're here in support of the fact—that it makes the best show. You just keep growing.

Ruppenthal: Yeah, I think it's amazing. I can remember one specific time when—you get into debates over how Sam's character would behave. In the motorcycle show, where they run into Jack Kerouac, we had a scene where he went to confront Kerouac at his cabin. I know Deborah and I had a sort of head-to-head on this one for one brief moment, where I had Sam coming in—'cause I took a pass at that one scene—and being more angry at him, and sort of . . . I wrote this scene with Sam coming in with a lot of anger and saying, y'know, "You're too passive, you've got to get off the sidelines and get with the program here and try to help these kids out. You talk about being involved and you're not." Then he left. It was a very angry moment, and we seldom see Sam that angry. We went around and around about whether he should be or shouldn't be.

We ultimately wound up toning it down. I think that's one of the times where I would have liked to have seen him go in that direction. It's a choice. The other scene played very well, also. It's just an interesting debate that goes on, that sometimes rages on around the office behind where, y'know, people discuss things, and then you finally have to just make the decision.

You only have one shot to film it; you can't film it both ways. Ninety-nine percent of the time, things come out for the best. We have this dialectical system going on, where it's thesis, antithesis, and then synthesis, and hopefully you're not too bloody to stand up afterward.

Thompson: He went to Harvard; that's why he talks like that. I had a scene changed in a script that we just finished shooting that Joe directed. No, it wasn't because of Joe, I don't even think Joe ever saw that. Don made me change it. It was at the end and it was very disturbing and very sort of violent and Don said he'd promised NBC a comedy, and so we changed it to something that was even more bizarre in my mind, so you'll have to see it. It's called "Moments to Live," but that one I would like to have had back the way it was.

Bridges: Usually my scenes that are cut have to do with undressing him. Where Sam's the bounty hunter, I had in one of the drafts, I had Sam asking Diane as she was about to go off to jail, "Was this for real?" She goes, "Yeah, this is for real," back and forth, back and forth, and had a—great big kiss, and then they leaped out on the kiss. We decided, "Wait, wait, wait, she's not in love with Sam, she's left with this bad-breath bounty hunter," and so we had to say, "Well, I'm going off to be a bounty hunter." So that was the one that I thought, hmmm . . . They always change. In the original draft of "Future Boy," I killed Captain Galaxy at the end.

I thought it was a good death! He died of a heart attack, but right before he died, he saw Sam as who he really was, and he knew that time travel was possible. So he went out on kind of an up note, y'know—but he still went out. I'm sure Richard Herd is very happy that I didn't do that.

Whiteside: In the Vietnam episode, there was one scene that wasn't able to make it time-wise that I really personally liked. When we shot it, those who had served in Vietnam were very affected by it. It was a scene after Maggie was killed and Sam had scooped her up and was running back with the rest of the platoon, which had now linked together. The camera's shooting down this path, with the platoon fighting off the bad guys, and the helicopter lands right in front of the camera, and you're now looking through the cockpit and they piled in carrying her, and the whole platoon, and the helicopter lifted off. For me, personally, it was just a scene that looked authentic. That was one that I hated to see go, but there just wasn't enough time to put it in.

Birnie: Me? I've had many sets kicked, many, many sets messed up. My biggest disappointment, I guess, is some sets that I've done have been very big, beautiful sets that the only thing that's ended up on TV is just this little square around a head. I guess it's why actors get their credits up front.

Q: Will Sam ever meet himself?

Thompson: We tried to do that once. Paul Brown actually wrote that into a script, and it got pulled out for some reason. It just seemed strange. I don't think we wanted to use it unless we had a really big story to build it around.

Ruppenthal: It was part of the chimp show, where when he was a chimpanzee, there was a scene written where the young Sam Beckett came in and met this attractive woman scientist who tried to sort of pick him up and was sort of unnerved about it and failed. The chimp kept trying to coax him along, really. "No, you idiot! She wants to go out with you!"

8

Celebrating Four Years of *Leap*ing

The following panel discussion took place at Universal Hilton Hotel on March 1, 1992 at the annual *Quantum Leap* convention. On the panel were Donald P. Bellisario, Scott Bakula, and Dean Stockwell.

Q: (For Scott Bakula) What was your very favorite character? As—in a comedic sense.

Bakula: In a comedic sense? Oh, boy! See, that's how bad it is, I didn't even do it on purpose. I think the first words my son is gonna speak are "Oh, boy." We're teaching him, we're working on that. You know, I—there was an episode that we did very early on, actually two episodes in the first year. Uh, the "Volare" episode, that Don wrote, is wonderfully comedic, I love that whole show. There was also "Play It Again, Seymour," which was a spoof of *Casablanca* and all those other ones. Those are two of my favorite comedic episodes.

Q: (For Scott Bakula) Do you feel the part that you've portrayed has gotten in some way deeper and more involved as the series goes on?

Bakula: Well, I do. I think Don's really a better person to field that, because he has a better sense of the scope of the whole thing, but I think as everyone has had input into the show, since we began, including Dean and myself, and Don and other writers, and people like yourselves, from all over, that mention things and talk about things, I think the show changes focus and moves, uh, it has a lovely quality of being different every week, so we can experiment with things. We've experimented this year with some shows that were "controversial." I think that that was a step for us in many ways, and I think those shows came off wonderfully well. So I think the show continues to evolve, and it certainly continues to amaze me, what these wonderful writers can think up.

Q: (ForDean Stockwell and Scott Bakula) Which episode or episodes have been the most difficult emotionally for you to perform?

Stockwell: Well, I personally don't find emotional difficulty as a performer. I don't get involved in it in that way, it's not part of my craft in acting. It's the real life we all know that affects me emotionally, the acting doesn't; although I use my emotions the minute the acting is done, I'm not emotionally any different than before I did the scene, or the show. I may be wiser at the end of the show, but emotionally, no.

Bakula: We're creating situations, or we're recreating them, where you get a glimpse into somebody else's soul a little bit, and, oftentimes you get it through another actor that you're working with in the scene. Oftentimes something comes out of me that I wasn't really prepared for, and oftentimes it comes out of him, although he'll say that answer, but stuff sneaks out.

You never know when that's gonna happen. You don't know. You can have the most emotional script, with the most intense story line, but if it's not fulfilled in all the areas . . . If by some chance it was to be miscast, or if it was directed incorrectly, or whatever, you can take a wonderful moment and kill it. So you never know, it's like you just find a gem sometimes. Those are quite often the most lovely things.

Q: Is there anything that you won't do with the show; with all the conspiracy things that are going on now, will Sam leap into Marilyn Monroe or JFK or someone like that?

Stockwell: I wish he would leap into Marilyn Monroe!

Bellisario: All Dean could do is look! It's really very difficult to leap the character Sam into someone that is a known character, because the one rule in creating the show was that we are going to alter history. Everybody who's ever done a time-travel show says you can't change history, you can't change history, that's part of the format of it, and we decided we could change history. So you have to leap him into characters that all of you don't know, because then you don't know what the real history is. If we leaped into Jack Kennedy in November of 1963, there's no way we can ever alter or change that. However, if we leap into an individual that you don't know, we can change the history any way we want. That's why we don't leap him into known characters, except maybe in a kiss with history, we might do it that way. Or in the movie.

Q: (For Dean Stockwell and Scott Bakula) How do you talk to the air when you're doing the holograms?

Stockwell: I have to talk to the air when we do what we call a blue screen, to make the hologram walk through things and stuff, and when I'm doing the blue screen I'm the only one there. We already shot what I see on a screen. So that's the only time I do it. Scott does it a lot, because whenever I'm there, and somebody else looks, I'm not there.

Bakula: It's hard. You get used to it; sometimes we are better at it than other times. With what we try to do in eight days of television, making new shows every week, it comes out pretty well. Dean's really excellent at it, so that helps a lot.

Q: How come you're, not supposed to tell Sam about Donna, and Sam says you do, and nothing goes wrong?

Bellisario: Because then it would ruin the series. If he told him, then he would—he would be plagued by that knowledge and then as he went from one leap to another he wouldn't be a free agent to operate as needed. So he can't tell him, and that means he can sometimes get involved with other ladies and still be— uh—moral. Sort of.

Most television series would never do that. We're the only one that had the opportunity to get him married and then get him out of it and keep him married, and I don't want to go into this any further. Next.

Q: (For Scott Bakula) Did you find directing harder or easier than you thought it was going to be?

Bakula: The directing was wonderful except for having to work with Dean.

Q: (For Scott Bakula and Dean Stockwell) Do you ad-lib your lines?

Bakula: I think it's safer to ask does Dean ever say any of the lines that are in the script. Those would be memorable. Go ahead, Mr. Funny. Mr. Never Can Finish A Scene With A Straight Face. Mr. Never Says What He's Supposed to Say To Me. Mr. Has To Have The Last Little Funny Thing On Camera. Go ahead!

Stockwell: It's so easy. I made, uh, one ad-lib about Styrofoam once that I think was my favorite. I said the stuff comes straight from hell! Yeah, we improvise from time to time.

Q: Is there any costume you'd really like to kill Jean-Pierre for?

Bakula: The pants in the "Glitter Rock" episode that weighed about thirty pounds, and ran. We had holes in them the entire time, but they looked fabulous.

Q: (For Don Bellisario) When you were getting the script ready for "Leap Back," did you have any discussion as to bringing Donna Alessi back, or bringing the brother Tom back?

Bellisario: It was controversial. Did we think about it? Yes. We wanted originally to bring Donna Alessi back in the part. She was not available; the girl that played that part was not available.

Bakula: No, that would have been a whole 'nother way to go in that episode. The force of that episode was finding out that there was indeed a woman back at home that I had not known about. I think if we had gotten into bringing the brother to New Mexico, why was he there—I was only there for a night, twelve hours. That would have been more than that episode could have; maybe next time it'll be a two-hour and then we'll get all that stuff in.

Q: How did you guys go about getting the parts? Was it like a big cattle call?

Bakula: It wasn't quite a cattle call. Don doesn't do those much anymore.

Bellisario: Dean and I had never met. Scott came in and read for the part, and I immediately felt that this was Sam and I didn't want to let my enthusiasm get away, because we hadn't made a deal yet.

Bakula: So he didn't.

Bellisario: So I kept quiet until he went out the door, and I went, "Yeah! That's him!" Then, Dean, I guess your agent called and said you heard about the part. There were a number of fine actors that wanted that part, and we took Dean. We're very happy we did.

Q: In some of your episodes, Sam looks up to the sky and is talking to someone. Who are you talking to?

Bellisario: He looks up and talks to someone? Well, he could be talking to Time, Fate, God. . . .

Bakula: Dean says now the star's up there, I'm talking to him.

Bellisario: He's talking to whoever you really want him to talk to.

Q: (For Dean Stockwell) If you had your opportunity, what would you put Sam into as a situation?

Stockwell: Well, that's funny. Even as you were composing that question, I was really reflecting on that very possibility! Donald just said something about writing an episode where he's a baby and I think he'd be great for it because that's what he really is, a big baby!

Bellisario: Scott will get his revenge, because the episode that I'm writing now to end the season, he leaps into Dean.

Stockwell: He'd better not botch it up!

Q: How do you go into the hologram door?

Stockwell: I go through the door—when we're making the movie, I'm standing there, the cameramen are there, Scott's there, everyone's there, and the director says, "Freeze," and everybody has to freeze, no matter what they're doing. I just go and run off. Then everybody says "unfreeze" and everybody starts to move again. Later on they just take that little piece of film out, when they all freeze, and I'm gone like that. Then they put the little light in for the door. We've got some really nice people that do that for us, with paintbrushes.

Q: If you actually had the ability to do what you do on your show, would you?

Bellisario: I'll answer, then I'll let Scott answer. I'm ambivalent about it. I would love to do it. I would love to do it because I have parents who are dead; I'd love to see them again. Scott, when he leaped back in "The Leap Home," found that he couldn't change his own family, until, of course, he got to Vietnam and saved his brother's life. So it's real ambivalent feelings about it on my part. I'd like to try it.

Bakula: I think there's a big part of me that attracts me to a show like this. I love the fantasy idea of the show. I would love to walk out of here into a little room and be in New York without having to fly across the country. Those kinds of things, if we could really do this, would be wonderful things to do. We get into a big discussion about fate.

Pratt: I think that, in our own way, we do change history. From the letters that we've gotten from people, just like this woman was saying over here, to teach and to share and a lot of people have gotten in touch with things from the programs we've been able to put on. So through Don's creation of this show, and Scott and Dean's performance of it, I think we've had the opportunity to change history. I'm proud to say that I hope we keep doing it.

Q: (For Scott Bakula and Dean Stockwell) How do you feel being in front of a camera?

Bakula: I like it. I've actually gotten to like it more and more. I feel very lucky to spend most of my hours in front of a camera with [Dean], and I learn so much from him. My roots are from the theater, and it was very hard when I first came out here to stand still, and I'm constantly learning new things. Everybody turns over in terms of cast every eight days; I've been able to work with a lot of wonderful actors in the last three and a half years. We've had some incredibly wonderful, gifted actors and they've given so much to us, and to the show and to you. I learn from them all the time, so I'm enjoying it more and more all the time.

Stockwell: I feel very comfortable, because I've been around them so long, so many years, so it's a very comfortable situation for me. More so than theater, say, but I'm comfortable with that, too.

Q: Does Al having had five wives make any problems?

Stockwell: Sometimes they're problems when they come up, but they get resolved quickly and I have to figure out how to employ a new development or a new wrinkle in the character in this cast. I have to figure out how to work it into what I've been doing all along. But everything that's happened so far has always worked wonderfully.

Bellisario: And the writers have to sit down and we have a bible and, y'know, Al has about five pages in there of his life history. And everybody has to always check and say where was he in 1968, and who was he married to when and . . . keep things straight.

Stockwell: Because I can't remember.

Q: (For Don Bellisario) On several of your programs you've written Vietnam themes and you portray a very positive image of the vet, so I was wondering if you were a vet yourself.

Bellisario: I'm not a Vietnam vet. I was in the marine corps for four years, and that was right before the Vietnam conflict, so I was right in between. But many of my friends were, and because of that I've adopted that theme.

Q: You've dealt with social issues—rape, the mentally challenged, things like that. Is there any social issue that you think would be too difficult to tackle?

Bellisario: No, I don't think there's any social issue that's too difficult to tackle. Networks may not agree with that, but I think we could.

Q: (For Scott Bakula) Do you have a background in dance or the martial arts?

Bakula: I have a wonderful instructor, named Pat Johnson, who has come in since a script called "Another Mother." He is most famous for the *Karate Kid* movies, most recently for the Ninja Turtle stuff. He's a wonderful man. And no, I have not studied formally, it's something I'd like to do someday. I attribute my kicks to playing soccer from the age of about five, and I also have had dance training.

Q: You have the unique opportunity other people don't have to be in other people's shoes. Which character or show have you learned the most from?

Bakula: I'm really a big fan of the show, okay? So I really learn something almost every week, about people or a situation in life, or something, an issue. I am continually being educated, and my horizons and my envelope is being pushed out all the time. I've been a woman; I've been black; I've been all these different things. I haven't really been it, but I'm forced to think that way, and I think if we all spent a little more time thinking like the other guy thinks, it would be a whole better place out there.

Q: (For Scott Bakula) How old are you?

Bakula: You mean me in real life, or Sam? Me, in real life—thirty-seven. Sam is thirty-nine; he was born in '53.

Q: (For Scott Bakula) Are you currently working on any movies?

Bakula: I don't have anything planned so far. I'm trying to get through this last three episodes of the year, and then I may not do anything.

Q: (For Dean Stockwell) What's it like working with Gregory Peck when you're only seven?

Stockwell: Gregory Peck is a man of great stature. He was, of course, very young at the time. But physically he's a commanding figure, and I was very little, and the image and impression I had of him was like a statue of someone of huge importance of some sort or another. I realize now it was his stardom, his magnetism as a star. I didn't realize it then.

The man who directed [*Gentlemen's Agreement*], Elia Kazan, directed many classic movies. He had a way of working with the actors that evolved from the famous Actors Studio in New York, Lee Strasberg and everything, which was the absolute opposite of the way I worked. I had a way of working even when I was six or seven. He was constantly trying to deal with me on this Actors Studio level and saying, "Feel this and think that your dog was dead, or something, or your mommy got hurt," or something, and I would have to sit and listen to him, and the minute he would stop—and I'd try and give him the impression, "Okay, okay"—and go to something else. I would just go and do it the way I would do it. I'd put my finger in the corner of my eyes to make a tear come, and come in and play the scene. I didn't need to do all that stuff, so that was a very tough movie. He's the only Method director I ever worked with.

Q: Is there going to be syndication of *Quantum Leap*?

Bellisario: It's going to be on USA (Network) cable. It's going on cable, and I hope that's going to get more enthusiasm for the show, and we've got some plans in the wings for some episodes that are going to be very interesting. Deborah Pratt came up with the idea of doing an episode that's animated.

9

Leaping into Controversy

Don Bellisario has purposely had Sam avoid leaping into many major historical events. Instead the series has focused on powerful stories of everyday people. Some of these "small stories," as Bellisario has called them, have fired controversy. Episodes in which Sam has leaped into a pre–Civil Rights Movement black man and a woman before "women's lib" were two of them. Two other episodes have come under fire.

Animal Rights and Wrongs

The first was an episode in which Sam leaped into a laboratory chimp scheduled to die in a crash test. This story set off both sides of the "animal rights" issue. Kenneth Gould of the Yerkes Regional Primate Research Center said that it was "evident" that animal-rights activists were "deliberately setting up" the episode.

A Portland, Oregon, animal researcher wrote to Bellisario and charged that the show was "a piece of propaganda for a small and fanatical group of people who are opposed to animal-based research." Before the episode was produced, Don Bellisario responded by saying, "None of that is true. This is not going to be a piece of propaganda." He said the story would have "proper balance. I'm not here to do an animal-rights show."

Paul Brown, the author of the script, said, "I was just looking for a story. We've always talked about Sam being an animal or something unusual. We thought about him being a dog, but that would be a stretch." Brown balked at the idea that the episode was set up in advance with animal-rights activists.

A spokeswoman for the International Primate Protection League said, "I have yet to talk to one animal activist who had even heard of the planned program until it was mentioned in TV *Guide*."

"I have no objections to both sides being shown," Gould of the Yerkes Center said. "But given the choice of an animal-rights advertisement for an hour, I'd rather have the whole thing scrapped." The episode was not scrapped and was aired; however, the controversy it generated was soon drowned out by a later episode in which Sam leaped into a gay military cadet contemplating suicide.

Suicidal Cadet

An episode in which Sam leaps into a gay cadet had been worked on since the second season, but it was a difficult subject and Don Bellisario had not been satisfied and rejected the idea at one point. The script was revised, accepted, and began production during the '91–'92 television season. Dispute was immediate. NBC wanted the episode pulled out of production as rumors increased that advertisers would boycott it.

At one point it was rumored that NBC demanded that Universal Studios pay the cost of lost advertisers. Critics called that "economic censorship." Both sides dispelled those rumors. "We had serious reservations about carrying the episode at all," said Rosalyn Weinman, vice president of standards at NBC. "Even if the program came to us fully sponsored, I would have sent it back as unacceptable." NBC did admit to threatening to withhold the network licensing fee if the show didn't pass inspection.

NBC's position drew support from an unexpected source, the Gay and Lesbian Alliance Against Defamation. The Alliance had originally criticized NBC's move, but supported it after reading the script. Richard Jennings called the portrayal of a gay cadet "negative and unbalanced." Bellisario, Deborah Pratt, and the other *Leap* producers have all said that was completely untrue.

At the time an NBC spokeswoman said, "We told them, 'Go ahead and shoot it, but we're not paying for it.'"

The script went back for further revision before it could be taped. NBC's largest complaint was that the cadet into which Sam leaps was too young. The producers rewrote the script with a twenty-one-year-old cadet and the program went into production. Also added was a gay track coach at the military academy, who Jennings called a positive gay character. Bellisario appeared on

Entertainment Tonight and once again declared that the story would present "both sides."

It was broadcast in January 1992. Only one thirty-second ad spot was unsold, and was used by Universal Studios to promote one of their feature films. Of the story itself, a television critic at the *Los Angeles Times* wrote, "Unfortunately, the hour was not as well executed as well-intentioned. The character of the track coach came across as an artificial and awkwardly imposed script convenience. And the telegraphed disclosure of his own homosexuality—along with Albert's unnaturally swift conversion to enlightenment ('I was wrong.')—contributed to one of those familiar, pat TV endings in which truth loses out to tidiness."

10

Leap Speak, One More Time

The following panel occurred on March 17, 1990, at the Museum of Broadcasting Festival at the Los Angeles County Museum of Art. In attendance were Scott Bakula, Dean Stockwell, Don Bellisario, and Deborah Pratt.

Q: Could you start by explaining *Quantum Leap?*

Bellisario: It's the only show on television that requires an instruction booklet before you watch it. When I pitched it to Brandon Tartikoff, he listened to me, looked at me, and then said, "All right, I want you to tell me that again in less than twenty seconds and so my mother understands it."

I believe his mother understands it, but I'm still trying to explain it to Brandon. At least he's still listening, because he renewed us this week. That renewal is due not just to the show and everybody on it, but also to all the fans and everyone out there who really loved it.

Q: A couple of weeks ago, Sam leaped into two different bodies in the same episode. Will there be more of that?

Bellisario: That episode was the first episode written after the pilot. It didn't air in that order because we thought we'd confused the people enough. They were really gonna get confused if he jumped twice in one episode. So it aired when we were in the black hole of hell on Friday night. Most people missed it. It will air again.

Q: In every episode, Sam has a mission to accomplish. Do you have any plans to write an episode where he fails?

Bakula: It depends on what you consider failure.

The Indian episode was an episode that was on the edge of that because even though he told me my mission was to help this man die, I believed that that couldn't possibly be my mission. So in a way, Sam learned a lot in that episode. Technically, I succeeded, because I got the man to the place he wanted to be for the time of his death, but it was a big step, I think, for Sam to realize that. I know that there's an episode that they're writing now where—actually the opener for next year and the one that Don's working on now—we deal with a couple of things that we would like to change in our personal lives. And the rules change depending on the day. There will be a book at Christmas. We try and change our own personal history and are unsuccessful, I think.

Bellisario: That's exactly right. The end of this season and the beginning of next season deals with stories where Sam leaps into a situation where Al is trying to get him to change something in his personal history . . . and we learn a lot about Al in that . . . and is unsuccessful. I'm only in act three, and since I never know how they're gonna end until I get there, too— and I'm serious about that, I never do—I can't tell you how it's gonna end, except that he probably will not be successful in what he wants. Then in the opener of next year, he leaps into himself at age sixteen.

Bakula: I would have been really disappointed if that woman had jumped off the ledge. There's something that's wonderful about the show that Don has written and about this guy, that he does succeed on some level all the time. We don't have a lot of people like that on television that express those kind of feelings and emotions every week.

Bellisario: We can fail at what he thinks he's here to do, what Al thinks he's here to do, what Ziggy thinks he's here to do, and he succeeds at that mission.

Pratt: He didn't get the girl!

Bellisario: I think that's true of us, too. I think sometimes we don't see what we're here to do. I think Deborah's written—she can answer that, she's written, I think, six episodes.

Pratt: Yes, I'm sure I will write more episodes. As a

matter of fact, we're shooting one that I've written now which is a fun love story on the *Queen Mary*.

Bakula: She's also written—and she won't toot her own horn—she wrote "The Color of Truth," which she won an award for last year. She wrote "Another Mother."

Q: Has Sam ever tried to walk through that door that Al goes through?

Bakula: I haven't. I ought to do that sometime. I don't think I can travel that way. He's a hologram and the door is his own image.

Stockwell: He gets to kiss all the girls; that's my door!

Q: I've noticed there's been a lot fewer references to historical events this season than there were the first season.

Bellisario: Well, we did two things. We did something that we had when we did the first shows called "a kiss with history," which is like the *Peggy Sue* thing—is a kiss with history, or where he performed the Heimlich maneuver on a man who turned out to be Dr. Heimlich! We'll have him throw a paper plate to a dog and have a guy named Frisbee watch it go by. Those are the kisses with history and they are a lot of fun and they are so difficult to come up with and—this is a terrible excuse—we're gonna put more of 'em in next year, I guarantee.

Q: During the first season, you were trying to leap Sam back. Have you given up that whole premise?

Bakula: We did an episode where we discussed that. I knew that I missed home. Al said something to the effect that "this is your home now, each place where you are, and you can't worry about getting back. If you get back, you get back, but you have to make each place and each family your family and your home." So that's where we're at in terms of that.

Stockwell: It would be a good thing to somehow touch back on that.

Q: Sam is something of a divine agent righting wrongs. Have you received much feedback from NBC and the public on this, and do you plan to continue?

Bellisario: We get feedback from the public that likes it. I haven't had any from NBC on that particular thing, I think they like it, too. Mostly what the public likes about the show is that they can sit down with their whole family and watch the show and get some moral purpose out of it and not be embarrassed by it.

Q: There was one episode where he was the mom and the little child could see him. . . .

Bellisario: The little child's in the audience and she happens to be our child.

Bakula: Troian!

Bellisario: I gotta give equal time to her brother, who was also in an episode.

Stockwell: That's another rule of time travel according to Don Bellisario. That certain individuals—kids under five, isn't it?—because they're on an alpha wave and are very pure, they can sense or spot the hologram. And animals.

Q: Are there any plans to expand the time-frame window? To go any further back?

Bellisario: No. No. No. I did not want to go back beyond his own lifetime, because once you start to have him popping into the Civil War, and on a ship with Christopher Columbus, and all that kind of stuff, it loses—this is really gonna sound weird—it loses credibility! I could buy when he leaps into 1953, 'cause I was there. I can't buy back beyond that.

Q: (For Scott Bakula) What's your favorite episode?

Bakula: I get asked that question a lot and I like different episodes for different reasons. I don't mean that to be a cop-out, it's just that each one is so different. I loved the "Jimmy" episode where I played the mentally retarded guy. I loved the "La Mancha" episode. I loved "The Color of Truth." I loved the Italian episode, and I loved the episode last year where I played Sam Spade, the detective. So I could just keep going.

Stockwell: I don't have a favorite.

Bakula: He likes the shows that he's in.
Stockwell: I like 'em all. I like 'em all.

Q: You said at the convention in January that you liked "Catch a Falling Star."

Stockwell: No, I love that, but that's not my favorite. I really don't have a favorite. I really like 'em all. I really do.

Q: Each episode touches life in such a positive way . . .

Bakula: Well, I think in a way we do that. I mean, when I played the mentally retarded man, I felt—and this is a weird thing to say—but the way the script was scripted, I felt very . . . very disjointed from everybody. I never was close to that cast. They did scenes, wonderfully scripted, where people would talk like I wasn't in the room. I do feel a lot, just without even thinking about it, of those people and their lives. I think that's what we try and do is that, then, when you're watching it that you get that sense, maybe a little bit, of what it's like to be an eighty-year-old black man in 1955 and treated like dirt. If a little bit of that comes through, then I think we're doing that.

Q: Does Dean's personality impact the way you write Al?

Bellisario: Does his personality impact? Well, you saw him tonight sitting here saying he has his last name and I'm saying I've got his last name. These two gentlemen both are very, very fine actors. Now, you expect to hear that from an exec producer, but I mean that, beyond what you normally say. Scott, what he just said a few minutes ago, talking about how he was disjointed playing Jimmy, that's a performance that you saw that he gave. Dean does the same thing. We could write Dean differently and he would perform differently. His personality does impact, the fun that he has, but he does give a performance. It's not Dean. He can give a serious performance, too. He loves to think he's a comedian, and he's going to give a serious performance in the one that I happen to be writing right now. Very serious performance.

Q: Can Sam die?

Bellisario: He can die. If you think about it, when Sam comes in—I don't want to confuse you all, but when Sam leaps in and bounces somebody out, if that person was hit by a car and they broke their leg and hit the street and then Sam leaped in, Sam would not have a broken leg. But if Sam leaped in and was crossing the street and was hit by the car, then Sam would have the broken leg. So that's the way we think about it when we're writing. And so, yes, he could be killed.

Q: (For Dean Stockwell and Scott Bakula) Since you two know the characters so well, have you ever thought of writing an episode?

Bakula: We've been really lucky and extremely fortunate to have terrific scripts and oftentimes you have a great desire to help the creative staff create.

Stockwell: Oh, we help 'em. After they write it, we try and change everything, but we're so busy doing one show after another that it's very difficult for us to sit down and say, "Well, let's take the time to try and write one." They're up there full-time writing, we're full-time acting, Don's full-time seeing over the whole thing. . . .

Q: (For Scott Bakula) Do you research your roles?

Bakula: The only time I do research is when it's something that I have to perform or do that I have no ability in my own life to do. I try and approach the show in a way that I come at each role in as a fresh manner as possible, without researching, because I want to feel for the first time, what it's like—as much as you possibly can—what it's like to be mentally retarded, what it's like to be black. I really try and avoid research and actor talk. I never talk this way! I don't! But to be in each moment as much as possible for the first time, and then I have a wonderful man, Diamond Farnsworth, the stunt coordinator for the show and my double, and he teaches me everything that I don't know and he makes sure that I live through each episode. He's great, he does a great job.

Q: Do you ever plan on sending him back to a situation from another angle or right after he may have leaped out? I know you did that in the Italian episode, but it wasn't quite the same.

Bellisario: Right. We—that's been suggested to us, and we really haven't thought about doing that, about going back again and seeing, being back in the same situation a little later or a little earlier and handling it differently or seeing the result. Right now—I'll be honest with you—right now we're trying so hard to make this show understandable out there to most of America that with exceptions like "Gloria," and where he came in as Jimmy, we have pretty well kept Scott being someone his own age, I mean—well, the old black fellow . . . but we haven't tried to go too far afield.

Q: Is there a line you draw as far as the extent he can change something, say prevent the Kennedy assassination?

Bellisario: Yeah, there is, there's very definite. The show does not deal with events that you know about that can be changed; for example, the Kennedy assassination. Nor will it ever deal with that. We deal with the personal lives and small stories about people and how they're affected. Since you don't know these people, you don't know whether that happened or didn't happen. It becomes very believable. If we were to go back and try to prevent something like the Kennedy assassination, we couldn't. The only way you could do something like the Kennedy thing is to have him leap into a situation where he was able to know about the Kennedy assassination, was on Kennedy's staff or something, and was trying to tell them, "Don't go to Texas, don't go to Texas." Finally, he convinces them and so somebody says, "Okay, we're not going to

Houston, we're going to Dallas." But then he's responsible for it! And he's caused it!

Bakula: Think of the letters.

Bellisario: So we don't wanna do that.

Q: In this last episode, you saved a woman's life, she went on and had kids.

Bellisario: When you get into time travel, everybody says, "Well, if you change something, there's a ripple effect." What we did with this show is say, "Right." We don't worry about it! You wouldn't be here if he hadn't jumped into some episode.

Q: The intro to the show as it exists now mentions that Sam can travel within his own lifetime. Assuming that he lives beyond the 1995 leap-off date, are there any plans to do any future time episodes?

Bellisario: Probably down the line we will at some point, because it would be an interesting way to do a story, especially with Dean's character, back—or forward—into the future. Not right away. I don't think this season. If we're fortunate enough to last, we'll start doing something like that.

Q: Why can animals see Al?

Pratt: Animals? Animals have no preconceptions. They take you at face value as who you are. If they don't like you, they don't like you. If all of a sudden you're their master and you're standing there, and you're not standing there the next minute, they're going to, I believe, have the ability to see you. It's the whole thing, based on, animals feel earthquakes. They can be back in the bedroom, and if somebody that's not supposed to walk in the house walks into the house, the hackles are up. So, yes, that's what that's based on. As far as children, again it's the same thing. Children have no preconceived ideas of who you are, they just see you for who you are.

Bellisario: It's difficult to fool a child; for example, throwing your voice. You can not throw your voice and fool a child under the age of, I think, two. The child will always look to the person who is throwing their voice, where an adult won't. It's amazing.

Q: In "Another Mother," Al says to the little girl, "I'll be back, I promise."

Pratt: It's interesting that you say that. That was such a sweet moment between the two of them, and there were a couple of shows like that, that, just as a writer, I found myself setting up. One of them was when Sam leaped in and ran into the first girl, the girl he almost married; the professor show. I'd love to bring him back as the second guy she almost married, as that guy, and he's gotta deal with the moral dilemma of: Does he let this woman marry this guy, or does he push her on to him?

Same thing with, uh, Teresa. In the sense that I would love to do a show down the line where Sam pops in as somebody else and Teresa's all grown. So, yes, I do hope to do that and I hope we're on more than long enough to have all those opportunities.

Bellisario: The one I want him to do is, I want to leap him into *Magnum*.

Q: How do you make the series survive? Do you get the Nielsens every week, do you have an idea of well how you have to do to survive?

Bellisario: Oh, yeah.

Stockwell: Oh, *yeah*.

Bellisario: Every Thursday morning at seven A.M., Harriet calls me with the Nielsen ratings from New York, which are the overnights. Then at twelve-thirty we get the nationals, and then we get the breakdowns, then we get all the charts, and yeah . . . we know what we have to do.

Q: So what do you have to do?

Bellisario: We did it. We're renewed.

NBC's been very supportive, Brandon's been a fan of the show. When we started out, we were in the mid-season and we were renewed with numbers that normally wouldn't be renewed at all, except that he had faith in the show and we had a lot of support from over at NBC, a lot of people that love the show over there. That's what's kept us going. I'm convinced this is going to be a major, major hit show when the rest of the world out there understands that it's really not a sci-fi show. Y'know, it really isn't. It's just the device to tell the kind of stories we want.

Q: Do you have a certain number guaranteed for next year?

Bellisario: Twenty-two for next year.

Q: (For Scott Bakula) Do you prefer doing music to just acting, having been on stage, do you prefer doing all different sorts of things? Will there be more episodes featuring music in the future?

Bakula: Well, we're doing an episode right now where we're doing the tango, which is a lot of fun, in parts of it. This is really kind of the role of a lifetime, because I get to do something different every week. When you're on stage, you do the same show eight times a week, but it's different every night. I love that because you can work on things constantly. When we do a scene, we don't have the luxury of coming back to it— very seldom do we . . . in all of our shows have we gone back and changed a scene and reshot it. So it's gone. But this is the greatest role. I get to do everything that they, anything they can dream up, we can do. Really.

Q: (For Dean Stockwell) Sam gets to be a variety of people. Do you find that your role is a little more limited, you interact with one person. What does that do for you as an actor, and do you hope to be able to interact with more characters?

Stockwell: Well, that's the definition of Al's character in this, he interacts solely with Sam. That's a challenge in itself. I found that I got very fortunate when I got into this show in being blended with Scott, because we get along beautifully and he's wonderful to work with. He's great. He really is. Plus, he has to work twelve, fourteen hours a day, every scene, five days a week, every show.

Bakula: I get a day off Monday.

Stockwell: I come in, say, maybe three and a half days a week, y'know. That's why I leave it to the young guy to do all the hard work.

Bakula: He gets the little computer toys, he gets the clothes, he gets four-day weekends. . . . (*audience laughs*)

Stockwell: Al seems to have a hell of a past tense, a very widely varied experience in his life. A lot of that comes up in the show and those are interesting things to deal with and to act. So I'm very happy. I like the concept.

Q: What's the most important thing you are trying to express through this series? And where'd you get the idea?

Bellisario: First of all, I honestly can't tell you where an idea comes from when you're creating a show. You sit down to create a show, you work in your mind on it, whatever you're doing. You go to sleep thinking about it, and the idea comes. I was reading a book at the time by Timothy Ferris called *Coming of Age in the Milky Way*, which was dealing with how man learned about the cosmos, how man deals with time, and how we're trying to find the start of the universe. It was a layman's book, but it was really about Einsteinian theories and the theories that we have now about quantum physics. It really had nothing to do with this, other than I guess that was a seed that got it started. I was also at the time toying with the idea of doing a series about a sort of mystical Indian, a young man in the Southwest, who . . .

What's the most important thing about it? I think the most important thing about it is that we can take someone from the nineties and the sensibilities that we have today and we can go back and look at what we were and who we were as little as ten, twenty, thirty years ago and see how far we've come and how far we have to go.

11

Quantum Leap Episode Guide

by Debbie Brown

Credits for *Quantum Leap*

<u>Original Premiere Date:</u> March 31, 1989

<u>Starring:</u> Scott Bakula, Dean Stockwell

<u>Executive producer/creator:</u> Donald P. Bellisario

<u>Co–executive producers:</u> Deborah Pratt, Michael Zinberg

<u>Supervising Producer:</u> Harker Wade

<u>Producers:</u> Paul Brown, Jeff Gourson, Chris Ruppenthal

<u>Coproducer:</u> Tommy Thompson

<u>Story editor:</u> Paris Qualles

<u>Directors:</u> Various

<u>Art Director:</u> Cameron Birnie
<u>Director of Photography:</u> Michael Watkins, A.S.C.
<u>Special Effects:</u> Whitey Krumm
<u>Costume Designer:</u> Jean-Pierre Dorléac
<u>Casting Director:</u> Ellen Lubin
<u>Origination:</u> In and around Los Angeles and at Universal Studios
<u>Maintained by:</u> Anita Kilgour
<u>Special Credit work thank yous to:</u> Ailsa Jenkins
<u>Special thanks to:</u> Jason E. Dzembo, Debbie Brown, and Kitty Woldow
<u>Honorable Mention:</u> Sally Smith

First Year:

<u>Title:</u> **Pilot Movie** (aka "Genesis")
<u>Leapdate:</u> September 13, 1956

<u>Episode Number:</u> 001
<u>Air Date:</u> March 26, 1989
<u>Writer:</u> Donald P. Bellisario
<u>Director:</u> David Hemmings
<u>Guest Cast:</u> Jennifer Runyon, John Allen Nelson, W. K. Stratton, Newell Alexander, Lee DeBroux, Larry Poindexter, and Bruce McGill
<u>Awards:</u> Emmy Winner: Cinematography: Roy Wagner

Although the project isn't ready yet, Sam hops into the Accelerator and leaps. As Tom Stratton, an air-force test pilot, Sam finds his memory Swiss-cheesed, with only enough left to know that he is not where or when he belongs. Al explains that the project has gone awry and that the only way Sam can leap out is by flying the X-2 to Mach 3. Instead, Sam leaps after saving his wife and child, only to find that rather than leaping home, he's leaped into Ken Fox, a minor-league baseball player in Texas, at the end of the 1968 season, where he must make the winning play in order to leap.

Title: **Star-Crossed**
Leapdate: June 15, 1972

Episode Number: 002
Air Date: March 31, 1989
Writer: Deborah Pratt
Director: Mark Sobel
Guest Cast: Teri Hatcher, Leslie Sachs, Michael Gregory, and Michael McGrady

As Dr. Gerald Bryant, a literature professor at the Ohio college attended by his onetime fiancée, Sam has to prevent an amorous coed from attaching herself to him and ruining her life. Despite threats to his job, Al gives Sam the information he needs to reunite his star-crossed lover with her father and, maybe, give himself a second shot at marriage.

Title: **The Right Hand of God**
Leapdate: October 24, 1974

Episode Number: 003
Air Date: April 7, 1989
Writer: John Hill
Director: Gilbert Shilton
Guest Cast: Guy Stockwell, Michelle Joyner, Teri
    Copley, Alex Colon, and Nancy Culp

Having leaped into Kid Cody, a boxer on the take,
Sam has to win the championship to fund a new
church for his trainers, a group of nuns. Sam must
face the bookie who counts on him to take a dive
in the final bout, and, with the help of several
trainers, streaking, and Al's appearance in the
ring to guide his punches, Sam wins the bout and
finances the chapel.

Title: **How the Tess Was Won**
Leapdate: August 5, 1956

Episode Number: 004
Air Date: April 14, 1989
Writer: Deborah Arakelian
Director: Ivan Dixon
Guest Cast: Lance LeGault, Kari Lizer, Marshall R.
    Teague, and Scott Fults

As a veterinarian in rural Texas, Sam's mission
appears to be winning the love of an heiress to

a large ranch. Sabotaged by another suitor, Sam fails and finds that his true goal was to save the life of a sick piglet, and to help an unnamed cohort with a task he's performing.

Title: **Double Identity**
Leapdate: November 8, 1965

Episode Number: 005
Air Date: April 21, 1989
Writer: Donald P. Bellisario
Director: Aaron Lipstadt
Guest Cast: Terri Garber, Michael Genovese, Joe Santos, Tom Silardi, Page Moseley, and Nick Cassavetes
Awards: Winner: Emmy—Hairstyling: Virginia Kerns

Though his goal as a Mafia hit man named Frankie is unclear, Sam follows a list of instructions, supplied by Ziggy, in an effort to bring Sam back to the Project. These instructions result in the Great East Coast Blackout, and rather than leaping home, Sam finds himself in the life of the Mafia don who's been jealously preventing a romance between Frankie and the don's girlfriend. Sam believes he knows his mission, and publicly announces Frankie's marriage to the girlfriend, putting himself in a position to call a winning Bingo number.

Title: **The Color of Truth**
Leapdate: August 8, 1955

Episode Number: 006
Air Date: May 3, 1989
Writer: Deborah Pratt
Director: Michael Vejar
Guest Cast: Susan French, Royce D. Applegate, Michael D. Roberts, James Ingersoll, and Kimberly Bailey
Awards: Lillian Gish Women in Film Award for Best Writing in a Drama Series: Deborah Pratt

In the life of Jesse Tyler, an aging black man, Sam must face discrimination in the South while trying to prevent the death of an elderly white woman. Actions motivated by his own belief in equality cause violent reactions, as Sam tries to convince one of the pillars of the community to change her views on racism and the futility of trying to change a society for the better.

Title: **Kamikaze Kid**
Leapdate: June 6, 1961

Episode Number: 007
Air Date: May 10, 1989
Writer: Paul Brown
Director: Alan J. Levi
Guest Cast: Romy Windsor, Kevin Blair, Robert

Costanzo, Holly Fields, Jason Priestly, Richard McGonagle, and Janet Carroll

As a high-school nerd, Sam is required to prevent the marriage of his sister to an abusive drinker, with the wedding only three days away. By drag-racing the prospective husband, beating him with a car that couldn't have won without nitrous oxide, Sam shows the groom's true tendencies.

Title: **Play It Again, Seymour**
Leapdate: April 14, 1953

Episode Number: 008
Air Date: May 17, 1989
Writers: Telepay: Scott Shepard and Donald P. Bellisario
Story: Tom Blomquist, Scott Shepard, and Donald P. Bellisario
Director: Aaron Lipstadt
Guest Cast: Claudia Christian, Willie Garson, and Paul Linke

With looks that could double for Humphrey Bogart, Sam is Nic Allen, a private investigator looking for the murderer of his partner and, if he doesn't find the answer in time, himself. The case is solved with a number of *Casablanca* references, and Sam launches a new pulp novelist along the way.

Second Year:

<u>Awards:</u> Emmy Nomination—Best Drama

<u>Title:</u> **Honeymoon Express**
<u>Leapdate:</u> April 27, 1960

<u>Episode Number:</u> 009
<u>Air Date:</u> September 20, 1989
<u>Writer:</u> Donald P. Bellisario
<u>Director:</u> Aaron Lipstadt
<u>Guest Cast:</u> Alice Adair, Mathieu Carriere, Hank
   Rolike, Warren Frost, and James Mastrantanio

As Tom McBride, a New York City cop on his honeymoon, Sam must save himself from a jealous, and sociopathic, ex-husband. To make matters worse, the Project's funding will be cut off, stranding Sam alone in the past, unless he can prevent the U2 flight from being shot down over Russia.

<u>Title:</u> **Disco Inferno**
<u>Leapdate:</u> April 1, 1976

<u>Episode Number:</u> 010
<u>Air Date:</u> September 27, 1989
<u>Writer:</u> Paul Brown
<u>Director:</u> Gilbert Shilton
<u>Guest Cast:</u> Michael Greene, Kris Kamm, Kelli
   Williams, Peter Onorato, and Arnetia Walker

As a stuntman, Sam is to save the life of his younger brother, while trying to convince the pair's obsessive father to let the younger son go his own way, even if it means going into country-western music, rather than following the family tradition of stuntwork.

Title: **The Americanization of Machiko**
Leapdate: August 4, 1953

Episode Number: 011
Air Date: October 11, 1989
Writer: Charlie Coffey
Director: Gilbert Shilton
Guest Cast: K Callan, Wayne Tippit, Leila Hee Olsen, Elena Stiteler, and Patrick Massett

As a sailor returning from Japan, Sam brings a foreign wife to a small town. He then has to fight against the prejudice of both a scheming ex-girlfriend, as well as his mother, in order to gain acceptance of his new bride.

Title: **What Price Gloria?**
Leapdate: October 16, 1961

Episode Number: 012
Air Date: October 25, 1989
Writer: Deborah Pratt

Director: Alan J. Levi
Guest Cast: Jean Sagal, John Calvin
Awards: Shown at Museum of Broadcasting Tribute to *Quantum Leap*, March 17, 1990

Sam is shocked when he learns he's leaped into a woman, Samantha Stormer. As a gorgeous secretary for an automobile company, Sam has to cope with sexual harassment by the boss, a suicide attempt by a roommate, and the effect his looks have on the lecherous Al.

Title: **Blind Faith**
Leapdate: February 6, 1964

Episode Number: 013
Air Date: November 1, 1989
Writer: Scott Shepherd
Director: David J. Phinney
Guest Cast: Cynthia Bain, Jennifer Rhodes, and Kevin Skousen

Although the concert pianist he leaps into is blind, a fact that bother his girlfriend's disapproving mother, Sam can still see. At least until an exploding flashbulb blinds him at the crucial moment: when he must rescue his girlfriend from a serial killer.

Title: **Good Morning, Peoria**
Leapdate: September 9, 1959

Episode Number: 014
Air Date: November 8, 1989
Writer: Chris Ruppenthal
Director: Michael Zinberg
Guest Cast: Patricia Richardson, Richard McKenzie, Todd Merrill, and Chubby Checker

Rock and roll is about to become big, but not in Peoria. That is, unless Sam, as deejay Howlin' Chick Howell, can manage to keep the radio station where he's employed from being shut down by overly conservative town elders.

Title: **Thou Shalt Not . . .**
Leapdate: February 2, 1974

Episode Number: 015
Air Date: November 15, 1989
Writer: Tammy Ader
Director: Randy Roberts
Guest Cast: James Sutorius, Terri Hanauer, Lindsay Fisher, Russ Tamblyn, and Jill Jacobson

Sam's task as a rabbi is to keep his sister-in-law from falling for a sleazy author and ruining her life. In the process he also helps the family recover from the death of their son.

Title: **Jimmy**
Leapdate: October 14, 1964

Episode Number: 016
Air Date: November 22, 1989
Writers: Paul M. Belous and Robert Wolterstorff
Director: James Whitmore, Jr.
Guest Cast: John D'Aquino, Laura Harrington,
    Michael Alldredge, Ryan McWhorter, and
    Michael Madsen

Since mainstreaming the mentally retarded is not
yet a popular concept, Sam must help Jimmy
LaMotta, the "slow" young man he's leaped into,
get a job and gain his coworkers' acceptance, to
prevent Jimmy's brother from returning him to the
institution.

Title: **So Help Me God**
Leapdate: July 29, 1957

Episode Number: 017
Air Date: November 29, 1989
Writer: Deborah Pratt
Director: Andy Cadiff
Guest Cast: Byrne Piven, Tyra Ferrell, Kathleen
    Noone, Ketty Lester, John Apicella, Stacy Ray,
    John Shepard, and William Schallert
Awards: Angel Award: Deborah Pratt

Though he can't remember much more than

habeas corpus, Sam finds himself the defense attorney for a young black woman accused of murdering the son of the most powerful man in a small Louisiana town.

Title: **Catch a Falling Star**
Leapdate: May 21, 1979

Episode Number: 018
Air Date: December 6, 1989
Writer: Paul Brown
Director: Donald P. Bellisario
Guest Cast: John Cullum, Michele Pawk, Janine Turner, Ernie Sabella, and Paul Sand

Sam leaps into Ray Hutton, the understudy for the role of Cervantes, just seconds before curtain time. His mission: prevent the drunken star from falling and seriously injuring himself during a benefit performance of *Man of La Mancha*. Sam isn't helped by the presence of his former piano teacher, on whom he once had a crush, and who now appears to have caught the star's eye as well.

Title: **A Portrait for Troian**
Leapdate: February 7, 1971

Episode Number: 019
Air Date: December 13, 1989

<u>Writers:</u> Teleplay: Scott Shepherd and Donald P. Bellisario

<u>Story:</u> John Hill and Scott Shepherd

<u>Director:</u> Michael Zinberg

<u>Guest Cast:</u> Deborah Pratt, Robert Torto, and Carolyn Seymour

<u>Uncredited:</u> Donald P. Bellisario (mirror), Paul Brown (corpse)

Sam leaps into a reknowned parapsychologist and must prevent a young widow from joining her husband at the bottom of a lake; he must also prove that she's not crazy, despite her claims of hearing her dead husband calling to her.

<u>Title:</u> **Animal Frat**

<u>Leapdate:</u> October 19, 1969

<u>Episode Number:</u> 020

<u>Air Date:</u> January 3, 1990

<u>Writer:</u> Chris Ruppenthal

<u>Director:</u> Gilbert Shilton

<u>Guest Cast:</u> Stacy Edwards, Raphael Sbarge, Darren Dalton, Brian Haley, Stuart Fratkin, Robert Petkoff, and Edward Edwards

Trapped in the body of Knut Wileton, better known as "Wild Thing," the typical frat jock, Sam must win the confidence of an attractive campus radical before she bombs the college's chemistry building as a protest against the war in Vietnam.

Title: **Another Mother**
Leapdate: September 30, 1981

Episode Number: 021
Air Date: January 10, 1990
Writer: Deborah Pratt
Director: Joseph L. Scanlan
Guest Cast: Michael Stoyanov, Olivia Burnette,
   Troian Bellisario, Allison Barron, Andrew Held,
   Larron Tate, Kevin Telles, Eric Welch, Terrence
   Evans, and Michael Kemmerling

As a divorced mother of three, Sam's job of preventing his teenage son from running away, never to be seen again, is made more interesting by the fact that the youngest daughter can see both him and Al.

Title: **All-Americans**
Leapdate: November 6, 1962

Episode Number: 022
Air Date: January 17, 1990
Writers: Paul Brown and Donald P. Bellisario
Director: John Cullum
Guest Cast: Richard Coca, Ruth Britt, Pepe Serna,
   Fausto Bara, and Robert Benedetti

Keeping his best friend from throwing the high-school championship football game, costing both of them their scholarship offers, Sam must also get their families to consolidate.

Title: **Her Charm**
Leapdate: September 26, 1973

Episode Number: 023
Air Date: February 7, 1990
Writers: Teleplay: Deborah Pratt and Donald P. Bellisario
Story: Paul M. Belous, Robert Wolterstorff, Deborah Pratt, and Donald P. Bellisario
Director: Chris Welch
Guest Cast: Teri Austin, Stanley Brock, John Snyder, Rene Assa, and John Shepherd

Protecting a female member of the Witness Protection Program from a Mafia hit man proves difficult for Sam, since the FBI appears to have an informant confounding his attempts to hide her.

Title: **Freedom**
Leapdate: November 22, 1970

Episode Number: 024
Air Date: February 14, 1990
Writer: Chris Ruppenthal
Director: Alan J. Levi
Guest Cast: Frank Sotonoma Salsedo, Leon Rippy, Gloria Hayes, and Tom Everett

Rather than saving his grandfather's life, Sam has to escape from jail and elude the police long enough to get them both to the reservation, where the old man can die in peace, at home.

Title: **Good Night, Dear Heart**
Leapdate: November 9, 1957

Episode Number: 025
Air Date: March 7, 1990
Writer: Paul Brown
Director: Christopher T. Welch
Guest Cast: William Cain, Marcia Cross, Robert Duncan McNeill, Deborah Strang, and W. K. Stratton
Awards: Mystery Writers of America Award: Paul Brown

Rather than saving the damsel of the episode, who supposedly committed suicide, Sam is the coroner trying to prove that she was murdered, and find out by whom.

Title: **Pool Hall Blues**
Leapdate: September 4, 1954

Episode Number: 026
Air Date: March 14, 1990
Writer: Randy Holland
Director: Joe Napolitano

Guest Cast: Shari Headley, J. W. Smith, Teddy
   Wilson, Ken Foree, and Robert Gossett
Awards: Winner: Emmy—Cinematography:
   Michael Watkins, ASC; American Society of
   Cinematographers Award Nomination: Michael
   Watkins

In order to help his granddaughter save a small
bar from the slimy loan shark holding a note on
the place, Sam has to play pool like a pro . . . with
a little help from Al and Ziggy.

Title: **Leaping In Without a Net**
Leapdate: November 18, 1958

Episode Number: 027
Air Date: March 28, 1990
Writer: Tommy Thompson
Director: Christopher T. Welch
Guest Cast: Jan Triska, Fabiana Udenio, Richard
   Riehle, and Phil Fondacaro

Sam remembers he's afraid of heights when he
leaps into a trapeze artist, whose sister wants
him to catch her as she does a triple without a
net. Dad is less than pleased, since his wife died
a few years earlier while attempting the same
stunt.

Title: **Maybe Baby**
Leapdate: March 11, 1963

Episode Number: 028
Air Date: April 4, 1990
Writers: Paul Brown and Julie Brown
Director: Michael Zinberg
Guest Cast: Julie Brown, Jimmy Ray Weeks, Travis
    McKenna, Cathy McAuley, and Charles Frank

Baby-sitting a kidnapped tot and a flaky, compul-
sively lying stripper keeps Sam busy as they cross
Texas, on the run from the legal father and a
squad of cops.

Title: **Sea Bride**
Leapdate: June 3, 1954

Episode Number: 029
Air Date: May 2, 1990
Writer: Deborah Pratt
Director: Joe Napolitano
Guest Cast: Beverly Leech, John Hertzler, James
    Harper, Patricia Harty, Juliet Sorcey, Tony
    Maggio, and Louis Guss
Awards: Emmy Nomination: Costume Design

Aboard an ocean liner, Sam must stop the marriage of a young man's ex-wife to a mobster. In
the process, he finds himself in one heck of a
mess in the ship's garbage compartment.

Title: **M.I.A.**
Leapdate: April 1, 1969

Episode Number: 030
Air Date: May 9, 1990
Writer: Donald P. Bellisario
Director: Michael Zinberg
Guest Cast: Jason Beghe, Susan Diol, Norman
   Large, Pat Skipper, William Shockley, Sierra
   Pecheur, Letitia Vasquez, and Dan Ziskie

When Sam leaps into the life of an undercover
cop, Al explains that his mission is to convince a
navy nurse that her MIA husband is still alive, and
to prevent her from marrying a lawyer she meets
on the day Sam leaps in. But a series of coinci-
dences causes Sam to wonder about the true
nature of his mission.

Third Year:

Awards: Emmy Nomination: Best Drama; Golden
   Globe Award: Dean Stockwell

Title: **The Leap Home**
Leapdate: November 25, 1969

Episode Number: 031
Air Date: September 28, 1990
Writer: Donald P. Bellisario

Director: Joe Napolitano

Guest Cast: David Newsom, Olivia Burnette, Hannah Cutrona, Mai-Lis Kuniholm, and Caroline Kava

Awards: Winner: Emmy—Makeup: Jeremy Swan, Douglas D. Kelly, Gerald Quist, and Michael Mills; Writers Guild of American Nominee: Donald P. Bellisario

As himself at the age of sixteen, Sam has the opportunity to both win the high-school basketball championship and save his family members from their sad fates.

Title: **The Leap Home, Part II** (Vietnam)

Leapdate: April 7, 1970

Episode Number: 032

Air Date: October 5, 1990

Writer: Donald P. Bellisario

Director: Michael Zinberg

Guest Cast: David Newsom, Andrea Thompson, Ernie Lively, David Hayward, Tia Carrere, Adam Nelson, Patrick Warburton, Ryan Reid, and Rich Whiteside

Awards: Winner: Emmy—Cinematography: Michael Watkins, ASC; Emmy Nomination: Dean Stockwell; Directors Guild of America Award: Michael Zinberg

As a navy SEAL in his own brother's squad, Sam must determine whether he is there to save Tom's life or ensure the success of the mission during which his brother was killed.

Title: **Leap of Faith**
Leapdate: August 19, 1963

Episode Number: 033
Air Date: October 12, 1990
Writer: Teleplay: Tommy Thompson
Story: Nick Harding, Karen Hall, and Tommy Thompson
Director: James Whitmore, Jr.
Guest Cast: Sandy McPeak, Danny Nucci, Davey Roberts, Erica Yohn, and Penny Stanton

Sam finds himself in one holy mess as a priest in Philadelphia, trying to help an alcoholic priest deal with a killer and the death of a young parishioner.

Title: **One Strobe Over the Line**
Leapdate: June 15, 1965

Episode Number: 034
Air Date: October 19, 1990
Writer: Chris Ruppenthal
Director: Michael Zinberg
Guest Cast: Marjorie Monaghan, Susan Anton, Kristoffer Tabori, David Sheinkompf, and Robert Trumbull

Sam is a photographer who must protect a fashion model from a growing dependency on amphetamines and a predatory manager's ambitions.

Title: **The Boogieman***
Leapdate: October 31, 1964

Episode Number: 035
Air Date: October 26, 1990
Writer: Chris Ruppenthal
Director: Joe Napolitano
Guest Cast: Valerie Mahaffey, Paul Linke, Fran Ryan, David Kriegel, and Donald Hotton
Uncredited: Chris Ruppenthal (mirror)
Awards: Emmy Nomination: Art Direction

Things do more than go bump in the night when Sam leaps into Joshua Raye, a horror novelist, on Halloween. Although Ziggy claims he's there to prevent the death of a church deacon, things get even stranger when two more people die without warning.
(*It should be pointed out that the B-word is spelled out here in order to make the Guide as accurate as possible. Please remember that we are trained professionals. The editors of the Episode Guide do not take any responsibility for the horrible consequences that will undoubtedly befall anyone foolish enough to say this episode's title out loud.)

Title: **Miss Deep South**
Leapdate: June 7, 1958

Episode Number: 036
Air Date: November 2, 1990
Writer: Tommy Thompson
Director: Christopher Welch
Guest Cast: Heather McAdam, Nancy Stafford, David A. Brooks, Julie Ann Lowery, and Hugh Gillin

As Darlene Monte, a contestant in the "Miss Deep South" beauty pageant, Sam must come to the aid of an innocent contender who faces disgrace when she poses for naughty pictures taken by a sleazy pageant photographer. As if things weren't bad enough, Sam must ensure that Darlene finishes third so that she'll go on to become a doctor.

Title: **Black On White On Fire**
Leapdate: August 11, 1965

Episode Number: 037
Air Date: November 9, 1990
Writer: Deborah Pratt
Director: Joe Napolitano
Guest Cast: Gregory Millar, Corie Henninger, Sami Chester, Ron Taylor, Marc Alaimo, Laverne Anderson, and CCH Pounder
Awards: Emmy Nomination: Sound Editing; Deborah Pratt (award unknown)

Sam leaps into a black medical student engaged to a white woman in order to ensure that he and his fiancée survive the Watts Riot together.

<u>Title:</u> **The Great Spontini**
<u>Leapdate:</u> May 9, 1974

<u>Episode Number:</u> 038
<u>Air Date:</u> November 16, 1990
<u>Writers:</u> Christy Dawson and Beverly Bridges
<u>Director:</u> James Whitmore, Jr.
<u>Guest Cast:</u> Any Steel, Erich Anderson, Lauren
    Woodland, and Michael Fairman

Leaping into magician Harry Spontini, Sam has to prevent his estranged wife from taking their daughter away from him as she files for divorce so she can marry her sleazy divorce attorney.

<u>Title:</u> **Rebel Without a Clue**
<u>Leapdate:</u> September 1, 1958

<u>Episode Number:</u> 039
<u>Air Date:</u> November 30, 1990
<u>Writers:</u> Teleplay: Randy Holland and Paul Brown
<u>Story:</u> Nick Harding and Paul Brown
<u>Director:</u> James Whitmore, Jr.
<u>Guest Cast:</u> Josie Bissett, Dietrich Bader, Teddy
    Wilson, Michael Bryan French, Scott Kraft,
    Mark Boone, Jr., and Joshua Cadman

As "Bones," a member of a motorcycle gang, Sam is an uneasy rider who has to prevent a Kerouac-inspired young woman from meeting her death on the road.

Title: **A Little Miracle**
Leapdate: December 24, 1962

Episode Number: 040
Air Date: December 21, 1990
Writers: Teleplay: Sandy Fries and Robert A. Wolterstorff
Story: Sandy Fries
Director: Michael Watkins
Guest Cast: Charles Rocket, Melinda McGraw, Robert Lesser, and Tom McTigue

On Christmas Eve, Sam leaps into Reginald Pierson, valet to a wealthy contractor who is in danger of losing his soul in an attempt to demolish a Salvation Army mission so he can build his "Blake's Plaza." Seeing a similarity to the Dickens's character, Sam and Al decide to "Scrooge" the greed out of the man.

Title: **Runaway**
Leapdate: July 4, 1964

Episode Number: 041
Air Date: January 4, 1991

Writer: Paul Brown
Director: Michael Katelman
Guest Cast: Sandy Faison, Sherman Howard, Joeseph Hacker, and Ami Foster

On a cross-country car trip, Sam, as thirteen-year-old Butchie, must contend with a sadistic older sister and a mother on the verge of running away from an unfulfilling marriage, in search of the feminine mystique.

Title: **8 1/2 Months**
Leapdate: November 15, 1955

Episode Number: 042
Air Date: March 6, 1991
Writer: Deborah Pratt
Director: James Whitmore, Jr.
Guest Cast: Lana Schwab, James Whitmore, Jr., Hunter von Leer, Tasha Scott, Anne Haney, Parley Baer, Philip Linton, and Peggy Walton-Walker

Billie Jean Crockett is a pregnant teenager who will make the second biggest mistake of her life—giving her baby up for adoption—unless Sam, as Billie Jean, can convince someone to help her raise her child . . . before he goes into labor himself.

Title: **Future Boy**
Leapdate: October 6, 1957

Episode Number: 043
Air Date: March 13, 1991
Writer: Tommy Thompson
Director: Michael Switzer
Guest Cast: Richard Herd, Debra Sticklin, George
    Wyner, Alan Fudge, and David Sage

Sam leaps into Kenny Sharp, better known as
"Future Boy," sidekick to Moe Stein, host of the
kids' show *Time Patrol*, who also happens to be
building a time machine in his basement. Unless
Sam can prevent Moe's daughter from attempting
to have her father committed, Moe is destined to
be killed as he tries to hop a freight train.

Title: **Private Dancer**
Leapdate: October 6, 1979

Episode Number: 044
Air Date: March 20, 1991
Writer: Paul Brown
Director: Debbie Allen
Guest Cast: Debbie Allen, Louis Mustillo, Heidi
    Swedberg, Robert Schuch, Marguerite
    Pomerhn-Derricks, and Rhondee Beriault

An aspiring dancer working as a waitress in a
strip club is in danger of being led into a life of

prostitution unless Sam, as "Rod the Bod," can convince her to audition for a spot in a professional dance group. But, since she's deaf, the choreographer doesn't believe she has the time to give the young lady the attention she'll need.

Title: **Piano Man**
Leapdate: November 10, 1985

Episode Number: 045
Air Date: March 27, 1991
Writer: Ed Scharlach
Director: James Whitmore, Jr.
Guest Cast: Marietta DePrima, Angelo Tiffe, John Oldach, Denise Gentile, Frank Roman, and Cherry Davis

Joey Dinardo is a lounge lizard on the run from mob hit men. When Sam leaps in, he's been found by his ex-girlfriend, and former musical partner, and now both are on a run for their lives from a killer who seems to know their every move. Scott Bakula's lyrical debut: "Somewhere in the Night."

Title: **Southern Comforts**
Leapdate: August 4, 1961
(Alternate Title: Love for Sale)

Episode Number: 046
Air Date: April 3, 1991

Writer: Tommy Thompson
Director: Chris Ruppenthal
Guest Cast: Rita Taggart, David Graf, Georgia
    Emelin, Dan Butler, Lauren Tom, Minnie
    Summers Lindsey, and Diane Delano

It's the best little cathouse in New Orleans. No,
it's the Gilbert Labonte Sewin' & Quiltin'
Academy. As the proprietor of this worthy estab-
lishment, Sam must prevent the mysterious death
of a resident who doesn't belong there.

Title: **Glitter Rock**
Leapdate: April 12, 1974

Episode Number: 047
Air Date: April 10, 1991
Writer: Chris Ruppenthal
Director: Andy Cadiff
Guest Cast: Jonathan Gries, Peter Noone,
    Christian Hoff, Michael Cerveris, Robert Bauer,
    and Liza Whitcraft
Awards: Emmy Nomination: Costume Design

Sam is a glitter-rock star in danger of being
stabbed to death after a performance, unless Sam
can determine who, from a growing list of people,
the real killer is.

<u>Title:</u> **A-Hunting We Will Go**
<u>Leapdate:</u> June 18, 1976

<u>Episode Number:</u> 048
<u>Air Date:</u> April 18, 1991
<u>Writer:</u> Beverly Bridges
<u>Director:</u> Andy Cadiff
<u>Guest Cast:</u> Jane Sibbett, Ken Marshall, and Cliff Bemis

It's the leap from hell, as Sam, a bounty hunter handcuffed to a wily embezzler who will stop at nothing to get away from him, has to deal with his captive, as well as his attraction toward her, despite her countless attacks on him.

<u>Title:</u> **Last Dance Before an Execution**
<u>Leapdate:</u> May 12, 1971

<u>Episode Number:</u> 049
<u>Air Date:</u> May 1, 1991
<u>Writer:</u> Teleplay: Deborah Pratt
<u>Story:</u> Bill Bigelow, Donald P. Bellisario, and Deborah Pratt
<u>Director:</u> Michael Watkins
<u>Guest Cast:</u> Jenny Gago, Julio Oscar Mechoso, Christopher Allport, and James Sloyan

"Just think of someplace far away" is the advice Sam hears as he leaps into Jesús Ortega, a Cuban-American being strapped into an electric chair. A last second stay of execution gives Sam just forty-eight hours to either prove himself innocent or fulfill his mission so that he can leap before the Big Switch is pulled.

Title: **Heart of a Champion**
Leapdate: July 23, 1955

Episode Number: 050
Air Date: May 8, 1991
Writer: Tommy Thompson
Director: Joe Napolitano
Guest Cast: Jerry Bossard, Don Hood, Deborah Wakeham, Angela Paton, and Rance Howard

The heart of a champion belongs to Ronnie, a professional wrestler, who will die if he competes in the title match. Sam, as Terry, his brother and new partner, must convince him of his hidden health problem, while avoiding his own health problem— the jealous wrestler-husband of a woman who has taken an amorous interest in Sam.

Title: **Nuclear Family**
Leapdate: October 26, 1962

Episode Number: 051
Air Date: May 15, 1991
Writer: Paul Brown

Director: James Whitmore, Jr.
Guest Cast: Timothy Carhart, Kurt Fuller, Kim Flowers, Robert Hy Gorman, and Candy Hutson

Sam finds himself the brother of a fallout-shelter salesman during the Cuban Missile Crisis, where he must defuse a potentially explosive situation as panic sets in on the night of John F. Kennedy's speech to the nation.

Title: **Shock Theater**
Leapdate: October 2, 1954

Episode Number: 052
Air Date: May 22, 1991
Writer: Deborah Pratt
Director: Joe Napolitano
Guest Cast: David Proval, Bruce A. Young, Scott Lawrence, Robert Symonds, Candy Ann Brown, Nick Brooks, and Lee Garlington
Awards: Emmy Nominations: Scott Bakula, Dean Stockwell

Leaping into Sam Bederman, a mental patient who is suffering from acute depression, Sam receives an overload electroshock treatment, which causes his Swiss-cheesed memory to be replaced by personas from previous leaps. Al, finding himself visible to the mentally absent, must try to complete Sam's mission, and convince him to take another shock treatment, in order to leap Sam out before contact is lost forever.

Fourth Year:

<u>Awards:</u> Golden Globe Award: Scott Bakula

<u>Title:</u> **The Leap Back**
<u>Leapdate:</u> June 15, 1945

<u>Episode Number:</u> 053
<u>Air Date:</u> September 18, 1991
<u>Writer:</u> Donald P. Bellisario
<u>Director:</u> Michael Zinberg
<u>Guest Cast:</u> Mimi Kuzyk, Amanda Wyss, Douglas Roberts, Robert Prescott, Candy Ann Brown, Jeanine Jackson, Dennis Wolfberg, and Deborah Pratt
<u>Awards:</u> Emmy Nomination: Dean Stockwell

Struck by lightning, Sam and Al find their roles reversed as Sam returns to the future, and to a long-lost love, while Al leaps back to 1945 to prevent the death of a returning World War II hero and his former girlfriend.

<u>Title:</u> **Play Ball**
<u>Leapdate:</u> August 6, 1961

<u>Episode Number:</u> 054
<u>Air Date:</u> September 25, 1991
<u>Writer:</u> Tommy Thompson
<u>Director:</u> Joe Napolitano
<u>Guest Cast:</u> Neal McDonough, Maree Cheatham,

Don Stroud, Courtney Gebhart, Peter Jason, Casey Sander, and Royce D. Applegate

A pitcher on a minor-league baseball team, Sam must decide if he's there to help a fellow team member, get his host back into the major leagues, or baby-sit the porcine team mascot, all while resisting the amorous advances of the women in his life.

Title: **Hurricane**
Leapdate: August 17, 1969

Episode Number: 055
Air Date: October 2, 1991
Writer: Chris Ruppenthal
Director: Michael Watkins, ASC
Guest Cast: Marilyn Jones, Tracy Kolis, James Morrison, Bill Erwin, Barbara Townsend, Richard Grove, and Marjorie Lovett
Awards: Emmy Nomination: Sound Editing

Sam meets Camille, and possibly a killer, when he leaps into a deputy sheriff in a small Mississippi town, lying in the path of a deadly hurricane.

Title: **Justice**
Leapdate: May 11, 1965

Episode Number: 055
Air Date: October 9, 1991
Writer: Toni Graphia
Director: Rob Bowman
Guest Cast: Lisa Waltz, Michael Beach, Fran Bennett, Dirk Blocker, Glenn Morshower, Lee Weaver, Jacob Gelman, and Noble Willingham

Sam must don the robe of a Ku Klux Klansman in order to save the life of an ambitious young civil-rights leader, who is trying to register black voters.

Title: **Permanent Wave**
Leapdate: June 2, 1983

Episode Number: 057
Air Date: October 16, 1991
Writer: Beverly Bridges
Director: Scott Bakula
Guest Cast: Doran Clark, Lela Ivy, Joseph Gordon-Levitt, and Harry Groener

Sam leaps into Frank Bianca, a hairstylist in leather pants, to prevent the death of a young murder witness and his mother, in Scott Bakula's directorial debut.

Title: **Raped**
Leapdate: June 20, 1980
Episode Number: 058

Air Date: October 30, 1991
Writer: Beverly Bridges
Director: Michael Zinberg
Guest Cast: Penny Peyser, Nancy Lenehan, Arthur
    Rosenburg, Matthew Sheehan, Amy Ryan, and
    Cheryl Pollak

It's up to Sam to try to bring a rapist to justice
when he leaps into the perpetrater's victim, a
young woman who may have been unwilling to
press charges against the young man—the son of
a pillar of the community.

Title: **The Wrong Stuff**
Leapdate: January 24, 1961

Episode Number: 059
Air Date: November 6, 1991
Writer: Paul Brown
Director: Joe Napolitano
Guest Cast: Carolin Goodall, Gary Swanson,
    Albert Stratton, Kim Robillard, and Peter
    Murnik
Awards: Genesis Awards (Animal Rights): accepted
    by Paul Brown

The fates make a monkey out of Sam when he
leaps into Bobo, an astrochimp who must avoid
succumbing to the experiments of an air-force
neurologist.

Title: **Dreams**
Leapdate: February 28, 1979

Episode Number: 060
Air Date: November 13, 1991
Writer: Deborah Pratt
Director: Anita Addison
Guest Cast: Joycelyn O'Brien, Alan Scarfe, and Bill
    Marcus
Awards: Emmy Nominations: Scott Bakula,
    Michael Watkins, ASC; ASC Award Nomination:
    Michael Watkins, ASC

It's more like a nightmare when Sam leaps into a detective investigating a gruesome murder. He may be next if he doesn't find out who eviscerated the victim, and his only hope is the victim's catatonic son and her husband's psychiatrist. The horrific flashbacks he's experiencing don't help matters much either.

Title: **A Single Drop of Rain**
Leapdate: September 7, 1953

Episode Number: 061
Air Date: November 20, 1991
Writer: Teleplay: Richard C. Okie
Story: Richard C. Okie and Donald P. Bellisario
Director: Virgil W. Vogel
Guest Cast: Phyllis Lyons, Patrick Massett, Carl

Anthony Payne II, Britt Leach, R. G. Armstrong,
Anne Haney, and Hal Landon, Jr.
Awards: Emmy Nomination: Costume Design

A devastating drought will be the ruin of a small
town unless Sam, as Billy Beaumont, "purveyor of
precipitation and maker of rain," can find a way to
make it rain, while keeping his family together in
the process.

Title: **Unchained**
Leapdate: November 2, 1956

Episode Number: 062
Air Date: November 27, 1991
Writer: Paris Qualles
Director: Michael Watkins
Guest Cast: Basil Wallace, J. C. Quinn, Claude Earl
    Jones, Don Sparks, Robert V. Barron, and Jed Mills

Sam and a fellow convict named Boone are the
defiant ones when Sam has to rescue his companion from a fifteen-year sentence on a chain gang.

Title: **The Play's the Thing**
Leapdate: September 9, 1969

Episode Number: 063
Air Date: January 8, 1992

Writer: Beverly Bridges
Director: Eric Laneuville
Guest Cast: Penny Fuller, Robert Pine, Daniel
    Roebuck, Anna Gunn, and Craig Richard
    Nelson

May meets December when Sam leaps into a
young actor in love with an older woman, who is
also an aspiring singer. If he can't boost her confidence and help her get her career on track, she
will face a "fate worse than death," returning with
her son to Cleveland.

Title: **Running for Honor**
Leapdate: June 11, 1964

Episode Number: 064
Air Date: January 15, 1992
Writer: Robert Harris Duncan
Director: Bob Hulme
Guest Cast: John Finn, Sean O'Bryan, Anthony
    Palermo, John Roselius, and Lisa Lawrence

As a track star in a navy college, Sam must
prevent the death of his ex-roommate, who
was expelled because he was gay, and who is
slated to die at the hands of a group of bigoted
cadets.

Title: **Temptation Eyes**
Leapdate: February 1, 1985

Episode Number: 065
Air Date: January 22, 1992
Writer: Paul Brown
Director: Christopher Hibler
Guest Cast: Tamilyn Tomita, Kent Williams, and James Handy
Uncredited: Harker Wade (mirror)

A serial killer stalks San Francisco while Sam, as Dillion Powell, a TV reporter, protects a beautiful psychic who's working on the case from becoming the next victim. The young lady is very clear of sight, as Sam and Al soon discover.

Title: **The Last Gunfighter**
Leapdate: November 28, 1957

Episode Number: 066
Air Date: January 29, 1992
Writers: Teleplay: Sam Rolfe and Chris Ruppenthal
Story: Sam Rolfe
Director: Joe Napolitano
Guest Cast: John Anderson, Susan Isaacs, Kenneth Tigar, Sean Baca, O'Neal Compton, and Jerry Potter

Sam finds himself in the life of Tyler Meanes, a teller of tall tales who faces death at the hand of an old friend in a shoot-out at high noon.

Title: **A Song for the Soul**
Leapdate: April 7, 1963

Episode Number: 067
Air Date: February 26, 1992
Writer: Deborah Pratt
Director: Michael Watkins
Guest Cast: Harrison Page, Tamara Townsend,
    T'Keyah "Crystal" Keymah, and Eric LaSalle
Awards: Emmy Nomination: Harrison Page; Emmy
    Nomination: Art Direction; "Eddie" award
    (American Cinema Editors): Jon Koslowsky

As a backup singer in a black, amateur girl group
Sam finds himself between the fifteen-year-old
lead singer and her father as he attempts to rescue
the girl from a sleazy nightclub owner's clutches.

Title: **Ghost Ship**
Leapdate: August 13, 1956

Episode Number: 068
Air Date: March 4, 1992
Writers: Paris Qualles and Donald P. Bellisario
Director: Anita Addison
Guest Cast: Scott Hoxby, Kimberly Foster, Kurt
    Deutsch, and Carla Gugino

Flying over the Bermuda Triangle, Sam, as the
copilot, must prevent the flight from returning to
Virginia, to get a seriously ill passenger to a doc-

tor before she dies. Flying through the triangle is riskier than it seems, and Sam, deprived of Al's help when the hologram fades out, must get them through alive.

Title: **Roberto!**
Leapdate: January 27, 1982

Episode Number: 069
Air Date: March 11, 1992
Writer: Chris Ruppenthal
Director: Scott Bakula
Guest Cast: DeLane Matthews, Alan Oppenheimer, Jerry Hardin, Michael Heintzman, Marcus Giamatti, and Don Gibb

Sam, as Roberto, is a tabloid-talk-show host à la Geraldo who, with an asthmatic rival and coworker, tries to uncover a mystery at a local chemical plant, a mystery that may prove to be deadly for his coworker.

Title: **It's a Wonderful Leap**
Leapdate: May 10, 1958

Episode Number: 070
Air Date: April 1, 1992
Writer: Teleplay: Paul Brown
Story: Danielle Alexandra and Paul Brown
Director: Paul Brown

<u>Guest Cast:</u> Liz Torres, Jerry Adler, Peter Iacangelo, Robin Frates, and Jack R. Orend

Sam finds himself behind the wheel of a New York taxicab, in the life of Max Greenman, a driver striving to win his own tag, a license to drive his own cab. His mission is aided with the help of a woman who claims to be a guardian angel.

<u>Title:</u> **Moments to Live**
<u>Leapdate:</u> May 4, 1985

<u>Episode Number:</u> 071
<u>Air Date:</u> April 8, 1992
<u>Writer:</u> Tommy Thompson
<u>Director:</u> Joe Napolitano
<u>Guest Cast:</u> Kathleen Wilhoite, Pruitt Taylor Vince, Frances Bay, Brian George, and Matthew Ashford

Sam is a soap-opera heart surgeon and the obsession of a love-struck, if somewhat deranged, fan. He must escape from the woman and her husband, who kidnap him for reproductive purposes.

<u>Title:</u> **The Curse of Ptah-Hotep**
<u>Leapdate:</u> March 2, 1957

<u>Episode Number:</u> 072

Air Date: April 22, 1992
Writer: Chris Ruppenthal
Director: Joe Napolitano
Guest Cast: Lisa Darr, John Kapelos

It's almost as though Sam were on vacation when, as Egyptologist Dale Conway, he gets to read hieroglyphics, search lost tombs, and, of course, visit Egypt. But between an encroaching sandstorm, computer glitches back at the Project, the suspicious deaths of the guides, and a 3,000-year-old curse to round things off, Sam has very little time to play in the sand.

Title: **Stand Up**
Leapdate: April 30, 1959

Episode Number: 073
Air Date: May 13, 1992
Writer: Deborah Pratt
Director: Michael Zinberg
Guest Cast: Bob Saget, Amy Yasbeck, Robert Miranda, Tom LaGrua, and Mark Lonow

Sam, as the singing half of a comedy team, soon finds that trying to convince two people that they're truly in love is no laughing matter, especially when one of them is the object of a sleazy casino owner's desire.

Title: **A Leap for Lisa**
Leapdate: June 25, 1957

Episode Number: 074
Air Date: May 20, 1992
Writer: Donald P. Bellisario
Director: James Whitmore, Jr.
Guest Cast: Charles Rocket, Jeffrey Corbett, Larry
    Brandenburg, James Walters, Terry Farrell,
    Anthony Peck, and Roddy McDowall
Awards: Emmy Nomination: Dean Stockwell

Sam leaps into one Al "Bingo" Calavicci to prevent
the death of his married lover. But when Sam accidentally alters history, and finds out too late about
her untimely demise, it could mean the gas chamber
for Al . . . and a whole new situation at the Project.

Fifth Year:

Title: **Lee Harvey Oswald**
Leapdates: October 5, 1957–November 22, 1963
(Alternate Titles: Leaping on a String; Leap to
    Judgement)

Episode Number: 075
Air Date: September 22, 1992
Writer: Donald P. Bellisario

<u>Director:</u> James Whitmore, Jr.
<u>Guest Cast:</u> Reni Santoni, Willie Garson, Natasha
    Pavlova, Elya Baskin, Donna Magnani, and
    Dennis Wolfberg

As a result of leaping again before he had a
chance to complete his original mission, Sam
finds himself leaping back and forth through the
life of Lee Harvey Oswald. Following the sole
assassin theory, Sam and Al attempt to prevent
Oswald's attack on John F. Kennedy. But with
each leap giving Oswald more control over Sam's
body, history seems doomed to repeat itself.

<u>Title:</u> **Leaping of the Shrew**
<u>Leapdate:</u> September 27, 1956
(Alternate Titles: Washed Away; When Venus Smiles)

<u>Episode Number:</u> 076
<u>Air Date:</u> September 29, 1992
<u>Writers:</u> Richard Okie and Robin Jill Bernheim
<u>Director:</u> Alan J. Levi
<u>Guest Cast:</u> Brooke Shields
<u>Awards:</u> Motion Picture Sound Editors: Automatic
    Dialogue Replacement editing

It's Robinson Crusoe with a twist when Sam
leaps into a Greek sailor stranded on a deserted
island with a beautiful young rich woman who
appears to be less than fond of both him and
their stranded situation.

Title: **Nowhere to Run**
Leapdate: August 10, 1968

Episode Number: 077
Air Date: October 6, 1992
Writer: Tommy Thompson
Director: Alan J. Levi
Guest Cast: Michael Boatman, Jennifer Aniston,
  Norman Snow, Gene Lythgow, and Judith Hoag

As a marine captain whose legs were amputated
after a mishap in Vietnam, Sam finds himself in a
veterans' hospital, where he must prevent the suicide of a fellow patient who would rather be dead
than face life paralyzed from the neck down.
Making matters worse, his wife seems incapable
of accepting the fact that she and Sam's host can
still lead a normal life, in spite of his condition.

Title: **Killin' Time**
Leapdate: June 18, 1958

Episode Number: 078
Air Date: October 20, 1992
Writer: Tommy Thompson
Director: Michael Watkins
Guest Cast: Connie Ray, Cameron Dye, Jim
  Haynie, Joseph Malone, and Dennis Wolfberg
Awards: American Society of Cinematographers
  award nomination: Michael Watkins, ASC

Sam leaps into a tricky situation as an escaped killer holed up in a house with a mother and daughter as hostages. Escape isn't going to be easy for either Sam or his hostages, when the real killer breaks out of the waiting room, stranding Sam in the past, destined to die at the hands of a vengeful sheriff.

Title: **Star Light, Star Bright**
Leapdate: May 21, 1966

Episode Number: 079
Air Date: October 27, 1992
Writer: Tommy Thompson
Director: Christopher Hibler
Guest Cast: Morgan Weisser, H. Richard Greene, Michael L. Maguire, Anne Lockhart, and Guy Boyd

Sam leaps into a seventy-nine-year-old man whose son wants to have him committed when he claims to have seen UFOs. Sam is kept busy as he tries to keep the family together, prevent the future drug overdose of "his" grandson, and avoid the sinister plans of the military, all before the next anticipated UFO sighting.

Title: **Deliver Us from Evil**
Leapdate: March 19, 1966

Episode Number: 080
Air Date: November 10, 1992
Writers: Robin Jill Bernheim, Tommy Thompson,
  and Deborah Pratt
Director: Bob Hulme
Guest Cast: Renee Coleman, Carolyn Seymour,
  John D'Aquino, Laura Harrington, Kristen
  Cloke, and Ryan McWhorter

Things are already on their way downhill when
Sam leaps back into Jimmy LaMotta. Despite
Sam's inaction, history continues to change for
the worse. The cause is unknown until Sam dis-
covers another time traveler on the scene, one
who's determined to destroy Jimmy's family, as
well as Sam.

Title: **Trilogy**
Air Date: November 17, 1992 (Part I) &
November 24, 1992 (parts II & III)
Writer: Deborah Pratt
Director: James Whitmore, Jr.

Part I
Leapdate: August 8, 1955
(Alternate Title: One Little Heart)

Episode Number: 081

Guest Cast: Mary Gordon Murry, Max Wright, Kimberly Cullum, Stephen Lee, Fran Bennett, Travis Fine, Meg Foster, W. K. Stratton, and Clayton Fuller (mirror)

A pair of unsolved murders mark just the tip of the iceberg when Sam leaps into a sheriff in a small Louisiana town. Rumors of a history of family insanity, the suspicions surrounding his daughter Abigail's involvement in the murders, and ghostly visions of his institutionalized wife just make matters worse.

Part II

Leapdate: June 14, 1966

(Alternative Title: For Your Love)

Episode Number: 082

Guest Cast: Melora Hardin, Mary Gordon Murry, Wendy Robie, Christopher Curry, Stephen Lee, Fran Bennett, Meg Foster, Travis Fine, W. K. Stratton, Beth Peters, and R. Leo Schreiber

Finding himself back in the small Louisiana town, in the arms of Abigail, now twenty-one, Sam must prevent an angry crowd of townspeople from lynching his fiancée, following the disappearance of a young boy whom she had been baby-sitting.

Part III
Leapdate: July 28, 1978
(Alternate Title: The Last Door)
Episode Number: 083
Guest Cast: Melora Hardin, James Greene, Parley
    Baer, Stephen Lee, Fran Bennett, Diana
    Bellamy, Meg Foster, With: W. K. Stratton,
    Kimberly Cullum, Lanier Edwards, and Heather
    Lauren Olson

Sam is an aging lawyer, recruited by Abigail, now
thirty-three, to defend her when she is put on trial
for the murder of Lita Aider, the woman whose
daughter Abigail was accused of killing almost
twenty-five years earlier.

Title: **Promised Land**
Leapdate: December 22, 1971

Episode Number: 084
Air Date: December 15, 1992
Writers: Gillian Horvarth and Tommy Thompson
Director: Scott Bakula
Guest Cast: Dwier Brown, Arlen Dean Snyder,
    Chris Stacy, Jonathan Hogan, Elizabeth
    Dennehy, Kellie Overbey, Lorinne Dills-Vozoff,
    Elizabeth Rainey.

Sam leaps back to Elk Ridge, Indiana, to help
save the lives of the Walters boys as they try to
save their farm from a banker with designs on getting rich from foreclosure.

<u>Title:</u> **A Tale of Two Cities**
<u>Leapdate:</u> February 25, 1958

<u>Episode Number:</u> 085
<u>Air Date:</u> January 5, 1993
<u>Writer:</u> Robin Jill Bernheim
<u>Director:</u> Christopher Hibler
<u>Guest Cast:</u> Mary Lou Childs, Jill Tracy, Ashley Peldon, J. D. Daniels, Shay Astar, Michael Bellisario, and Larry Manetti

As a horse-playing, traveling brush salesman, Sam finds himself with two wives and two families. Although Ziggy predicts that Sam's mission is to choose between the two lives, the choice is made more difficult by the fact that there's only a fifty-fifty chance that he'll choose the right one. As if things weren't bad enough, Sam finds that his penniless host owes a pair of bookies some big bucks.

<u>Title:</u> **Liberation**
<u>Leapdate:</u> October 19, 1968

<u>Episode Number:</u> 086
<u>Air Date:</u> January 12, 1993
<u>Writers:</u> Chris Abbott and Deborah Pratt
<u>Director:</u> Bob Hulme
<u>Guest Cast:</u> Max Gail, Deborah Van Valkenburgh, Stephen Mills, Bill Calvert, and Megyn Price

Leaping into a housewife and mother of two on

the verge of women's lib, Sam must prevent the death of his daughter during a sit-in, while convincing the girl's father that his marriage can survive a liberated wife and daughter.

Title: **Dr. Ruth**
Leapdate: April 25, 1985

Episode Number: 087
Air Date: January 19, 1993
Writer: Robin Hill Bernheim
Director: Stuart Margolin
Guest Cast: Peter Spears, Anita Barone, James McDonnell, Robyn Lively, and Dr. Ruth Westheimer

While Sam is in 1985, running her radio talk show, playing matchmaker to her producers, and trying to help a young secretary who's being sexually harassed by her boss, Dr. Ruth Westheimer spends her time in the waiting room, counseling Al on his feelings toward his five wives, as well as his relationship with Tina.

Title: **Blood Moon**
Leapdate: March 10, 1975

Episode Number: 088
Air Date: February 9, 1993

<u>Writer:</u> Tommy Thompson
<u>Director:</u> Alan J. Levi
<u>Guest Cast:</u> Ian Buchanan, Deborah Maria Moore,
  Shae D'Lyn, Rod Loomis

As an eccentric, possibly vampiric, artist just outside of London, Sam must bear with Al's supersti-
tions, while trying to prevent the death of his
host's young wife at the hands of a couple who
are performing a sacrificial ceremony in honor of
the "blood moon."

<u>Title:</u> **Return**
<u>Leapdate:</u> October 8, 1956
(Alternate Titles: And Forgive Us Our Sins; The
  Evil Men Do)

<u>Episode Number:</u> 089
<u>Air Date:</u> February 23, 1993
<u>Writer:</u> Richard C. Okie
<u>Director:</u> Harvey Laidman
<u>Guest Cast:</u> Renee Coleman, Carolyn Seymour,
  Tristan Tait, Paul Scherrer, Bojesse
  Christopher, Michael Manasseri, and Neil
  Patrick Harris

As Arnold Watkins, better known as the Midnight
Marauder, Sam has to persuade a fraternity to
stop using chicken races as a part of their hazing
ceremonies, while Al tries to convince Arnold to
stop trying to get himself killed in retaliation for

his parents' deaths twelve years earlier. When Alia, the evil leaper, appears on the scene, Sam becomes determined to take her with him when he leaps.

Title: **Revenge**
Leapdate: September 16, 1987

Episode Number: 090
Air Date: February 23, 1993
Writer: Deborah Pratt
Director: Debbie Allen
Guest Cast: Renee Coleman, Carolyn Seymour, Hinton Battle, Rosana DeSoto, Katherine Cortez, Maggie Roswell, Sam Scarber, and Barbara Montgomery

Having simo-leaped, both Sam and Alia find themselves trapped in a woman's prison, accused of murdering a fellow inmate. Their efforts to unmask the real killer are not their top priority as the two attempt to keep Alia's location hidden from her observer, Zoey, who leaps into the same place and time, determined to make Alia pay for her betrayal.

Title: **Goodbye, Norma Jean**
Leapdate: April 4, 1960

Episode Number: 091

Air Date: March 2, 1993
Writer: Richard C. Okie
Director: Christopher Hibler
Guest Cast: Susan Griffiths, Liz Vassey, Joris
    Stuyck, and Stephen Root

As chauffeur to Marilyn Monroe, Sam must try to
prevent Marilyn's tragic death. But when a well-
meaning plan backfires, it could mean the end of
Marilyn's career, even if her life is saved.

Title: **The Beast Within**
Leapdate: November 6, 1972

Episode Number: 092
Air Date: March 16, 1993
Writer: John D'Aquino
Director: Gus Trikonis
Guest Cast: Pat Skipper, Eileen Seeley, Sean
    Gregory Sullivan, and David Tom

Sam leaps into Henry Adams, one of a trio of
friends who fought in Vietnam and came home
each with their own personal scars and the memory of a lost buddy. He has to save the life of a
friend, Roy, as well as of a young boy, Daniel, who
ventures into the woods of Washington looking
for proof of Bigfoot.

Title: **The Leap Between the States**
Leapdate: September 20, 1862

Episode Number: 093
Air Date: March 30, 1993
Writer: Richard C. Okie
Director: David Hemmings
Guest Cast: Kate McNeil, Geoffrey Lower, Michael
    D. Roberts, and Neil Giuntoli

In a bizarre twist of a genetic coil, Sam leaps into
his great-grandfather, Captain John Beckett, during the Civil War. He must not interfere with his
ancestor's romance with a riled Southern belle
named Olivia. He must also avoid being hanged
as a Yankee dog by some home-guard
Confederate soldiers.

Title: **Memphis Melody**
Leapdate: July 3, 1954

Episode Number: 094
Air Date: April 20, 1993
Writer: Robin Jill Bernheim
Director: James Whitmore, Jr.
Guest Cast: Mary Elizabeth McGlynn, John
    Scott Clough, Lisa Jane Persky, Garn
    Stephans, Gregory Itzin, John Boyd West, Eric
    Bruskotter, Frazer Smith, Melissa Bernheim,
    and Stephanie Scott

Sam swivels his hips into Elvis Presley, mere days before he is discovered. Along with making sure that Elvis does become the King, Sam must help Sue Anne, a local songbird, from being trapped in a not-so-gilded cage of marriage.

Title: **Mirror Image**
Leapdate: August 8, 1953

Episode Number: 095
Air Date: May 5, 1993
Writer: Donald P. Bellisario
Director: James Whitmore, Jr.
Guest Cast: Bruce McGill, John D'Aquino, Richard Herd, W. Morgan Sheppard, Stephan McHatrie, Mike Genovese, Susan Diol, Dan Butler, Dennis Wolfberg, Kevin McDermott, Ferdinand Carangelo, Brad Silverman, J. D. Daniels, and Michael Bellisario

Sam lands in a not-so-ordinary bar in a coal-mining town, where strange things are happening and familiar people don't know him. With the help of another Al, he still has something to set right . . . or is there more than one thing he needs to change?

12

Two Tributes to *Quantum Leap*

Sally Smith

On Easter of 1989 I watched the first episode of
Quantum Leap. I loved the show, but never dreamed it
would lead me to a haunted house, a mental hospital,
a brothel, or a jail. I saw these and other sets on my
several visits to watch the filming of the show.

Nor could I have imagined that the show would
bring me into contact with the nicest, most talented,
and hardest-working bunch of people I've ever met. The
only thing better than watching *Quantum Leap* on TV
was watching it being made.

Quantum Leap was a place where:

- the number one sport was picking on the star,
  and Scott didn't mind;
- the director's fiancée baked oatmeal-raisin
  cookies for the entire crew;

- after working together for eighty hours a week, the star and crew played softball together on the weekends;
- a set simulating live TV in the 1950s prodded Dean Stockwell into reminiscing about doing live TV in the fifties;
- you could meet Dean's mother, and producer Chris Ruppenthal's sister, girlfriend, and agent, or maybe a former guest star come back just to visit, because they'd had so much fun;
- writers actually liked what the actors did with the scripts, most of the time.

It was a place where you could stand with two of the guest stars, and watch a man spray-paint a goat. They had a poorly trained one that was the right color, and a better-behaved, but wrong-color goat; hence the spray paint for an extremely nonchalant goat.

They shared running gags. Scott and Dean rehearsed for "Miss Deep South" by singing "Cuando la Gusta" and doing the cha-cha. They kept singing the song almost every day for the rest of the season. Whenever silence fell on the set, you could count on one of them breaking it with that song. When they quit, the crew picked up where they left off.

Emotional episodes brought out silliness to counteract the seriousness. At one point during the filming of "Last Dance Before an Execution," Scott sat on the bed in the death-row cell and told Dean, "You are *so* full of it, y'know?" Later, Scott told Dean that growing up in the sixties had made Dean paranoid.

The cell door kept popping open when Scott leaned on it, so one time he ran through it and down the hallway, yelling, "I'm free!" causing the crew to cheer. "Show's over! He's out, that's a wrap!"

To relieve the tension after a rough scene in this episode, Scott said, "Remember, we're making a comedy here. A musical comedy." He then sang, "Shout hallelujah, c'mon get happy, we're gonna fry this guy today. . . ."

Everyone, crew and staff, demonstrated genuine wit. The set of "Southern Comforts" proved to be no exception. I told producer/director Chris Ruppenthal that supervising all the beautiful women in lingerie must be difficult. He shook his head and, with an evil grin, replied, "Yeah, it's really rough. Sometimes I have to rehearse with them at night. . . ."

Stunt coordinator Richard "Diamond" Farnsworth came by. I asked how he acquired the nickname Diamond. With a *big* grin, he said, "Cause I'm a girl's best friend!" I walked into that one!

Don Bellisario also dropped by. As he left, cinematographer Michael Watkins told him, "You get to go outside, into the sunlight, with birds . . . I'm gonna stay in here and turn into a bat and hang from the rafters."

During a fight scene, Sam slammed into a wall. Diamond asked Scott, "You wanna take that on your shoulder and not your face, Scott? We can't have you hurt." Scott replied, "Oh, sure," grinned, turned to the crew, and said, "I don't know, you guys want a week off?" while pantomiming a concussion. Script supervisor Winnie Rich meekly asked, "You'd do that for us?"

It got cold in the soundstage late that night, so I asked the director, "Chris, I'm freezing, can I please wear your jacket?" He said, "Sure, just take it off my chair." I then reflected that not only was I in a

Hollywood bordello, but I was now wearing strange men's clothes!

Clothes figured in another incident. One day I wore a *Battlestar Galactica* jacket to watch dailies with the writers. Chris Ruppenthal pretended to be incredulous and derisive, saying, "What is this, *Battle Galactica*? This is *Quantum Leap*!" I replied with mock whining, saying, "I don't have anything *Quantum Leap* to wear! This is the closest I could get. Besides, I wanted to complain to Jean-Pierre about this jacket. It doesn't have any pockets. Whoever heard of a flight jacket without pockets?"

Chris looked authoritatively at Tommy Thompson, then said, "There are no pockets in the future." Tommy nodded agreement, and said, "That's right, in the future there are no pockets."

Toward the end of the third season, I told Scott, "Get some sleep over hiatus!" He laughed, and asked, "Sleep? What's sleep?" I said, "You've forgotten, huh?" He said, "I'm going to sleep in April. Bye."

When I saw him again at the beginning of the fourth season, I said accusingly, "You lied to me." A puzzled, hurt-looking Scott asked, "What? No. I never lied to you."

I said, "Yes you did. You told me you were going to rest over hiatus and you went and did two movies!" while poking him in the chest. Scott laughed and said, "Yeah, so I did. So I lied. I'm a liar. So sue me."

One day between shots, Don came onto the set to talk to Scott. They began the eternal "is it Sam's whole body or just his mind leaping" discussion. Don insisted it was his body; Scott argued for just his mind or soul.

As they talked, and each gave examples from episodes, their voices grew louder. The assistant director yelled, "Quiet!" because they were disrupting the rehearsal, then turned to see who was making the noise. Seeing them, he just shrugged.

Scott and Don noticed their audience and raised their voices still louder. Don grew ever more Italian as Scott cranked up his Stage Actor Voice. Dean looked over and shook his head as if to say, "See what I have to work with?"

The set came to a standstill. Everyone watched and laughed. Scott retreated as Don won points. Finally, in mock exasperation, Scott demanded, "Then how come . . ." noting a little inconsistency Don couldn't explain away.

Don gave him a big "gotcha, sucker!" grin, waited two beats, then countered, "Because I wanted it that way!"

The set roared with laughter. Scott threw his hands up and said, "Well, why didn't you say so in the first place? That I can understand! We could have saved this whole deal!" Don giggled in triumph as everyone laughed harder.

It wasn't all fun and games. There were intense moments, such as when I stood behind the mirror in "Shock Theater" watching Scott-as-Sam-as-Jimmy clinging to Brad Silverman, Jimmy's mirror image, as we both cried. Some crew members sniffled, while others held their breath, for both takes.

Later that day Al's pleading to Sam at the end of the episode earned Dean a stunned silence. And a round of applause from the crew.

Don arrived and quietly said, "I have some news." Silence fell as he announced, "We've been picked up." The crew cheered, then went back to work on the electroshock scenes.

The third-season wrap party was held in a bowling alley

the next day. The cast, crew, and staff actually went bowling. Several had *Quantum Leap* bowling shirts. Those not bowling danced, talked, or drank malteds, completely free of fast-lane Hollywood pretensions!

The crew got bottles of Dom Pérignon for all the Emmy nominees and gave their own awards. Assistant Director Paul Sirmons, clad in a tuxedo T-shirt, read off the introductions, mostly of a "roast" nature. His intro for Don was the best.

It purported to be a transcript of Don pitching QL to NBC head Brandon Tartikoff. I'll paraphrase the real intro, as it was much longer and funnier.

"Okay, there's this guy, see, he leaps into other people's lives, but we always see him as him except when he looks into a mirror, then we see who he's replaced, but all the other people see him as the other person. Then there's this other guy, who nobody but our hero can see, except the audience can; oh, and animals and children under five, when it's convenient. But our hero can't touch him, 'cause he's a hologram. And there's these other two guys named Ziggy and Gooshie, who we never see, but they're great. So our hero is there to put things right that went wrong, and as soon as he does that, he leaps into somebody else. And here's the best part: There are no standing sets and lots of special effects, so it's going to be really expensive!" Don said the speech was frighteningly close to the truth.

Don thanked everyone from Scott and Dean on down, saying that this was the best show he'd ever worked on. Dean said he didn't care if he won, as long as Scott and the show did. Scott gave a very emotional speech saying this mock ceremony meant more than winning because it was from the people he cared about.

The feelings were reciprocated. Two days after Scott won his Golden Globe award, the first words anyone on the crew and staff said to me were, "Isn't it great about Scott?"

Dean asked if we were going to the convention. I said, "Yeah. With your star," the one whose fans got him on the Hollywood Walk of Fame. He shrugged and grinned, saying, "Yeah, I'm gonna be down there on the sidewalk. People are gonna be stepping on me, spitting gum on me, doing this," and flicked some ashes off his cigar. Nonetheless, he felt honored.

Then there were the small joys:

- being sworn to secrecy after learning about upcoming plot twists while watching scenes;
- playing with Ziggy's handlink and listening to Dean make appropriate noises when he did the same;
- the endless spectacle of food provided by craft service wizard Louis;
- the sheer pleasure of watching a talented group of professionals working together to create something wonderful, despite too little time and money.

Much more sticks in my mind. The pop-culture thrills of being interviewed by USA *Today* and TV *Guide*. Watching Dean Stockwell and Dennis Hopper—two icons of the wild sixties—wearing suits and discussing their kids during a break from being part of the security team at Dean's star ceremony. Being at Dean's on-set birthday party, and getting to bring my husband, who shares the birthday. Attending the screenings and question-and-answer sessions. Working the first two conventions, and cochairing the third, only a month after the earthquake!

I want to thank those not mentioned, especially Deborah Pratt, prop guys Vaughn and Billy, makeup ace Jeremy Swan, Michael Watkins and his whole camera crew, Paul Brown, Tommy Thompson and Beverly Bridges, Michael Zinberg and Harker Wade, Rosemary Tarquinio, and Harriet Marguilies. It is a pleasure and a privilege to know these people and have been a small part of the big fun.

I still try to keep in touch with the folks I met. If any are reading this, rest assured that even if you haven't heard from me lately, I will never forget any of you. It was a fantastic ride. Thanks for letting me tag along!

Anita Kilgour

I was hooked the first time I watched *Quantum Leap*. Raised on storybook heroes such as Don Quixote, Robin Hood, and the Three Musketeers, I immediately identified with Sam and Al.

These intelligent men did what needed to be done, when most of television offered brain pablum and antiheroes. This show offered intelligent writing and characters acceptable as real people.

Sam was what many of us wished we could be, but that's what a hero is for, to provide an ideal. We could join our heroes in their quest to "put right what once went wrong."

Quantum Leap also helped me make new friends. The Internet and a great lady named Sally Smith got me on an electronic mailing list. That list led me to the man I married. I always wanted to thank *QL*.

Three years ago my fiancé and I were just words on a screen to each other. He was working on his PhD in the U.S. and I was working in Canada. One day, much to my own surprise, I decided to go visit him in person. We'd been friends for almost two years via the net, but I'd never met him face-to-face. I had seen a video tape of him, but that was all.

My roommate thought it was a great idea and helped me get on the train to meet him. I have always thought something was odd about our actions that day. She would never have bullied me onto the train.

I saw him when I got off the train. Paul leaned against a post, reading a book. God, Fate, or Time must have had plans for us. I suddenly reached up, pulled the book down, said, "I've been waiting to do this all day," then kissed him. It was as if a bell rang inside my head. The universe "clicked" into place. This was who I was meant to be with.

Whatever might have been wrong was now right. The look on his face told me that I wasn't the only one who felt that way. We fell in love overnight. Now we're less than a year away from being man and wife.

Sam still travels the gateways of time in our hearts, putting right what once went wrong. He instills honor, duty, loyalty, thirst for knowledge and freedom, and love in all of us. These are too easily forgotten in our world.

Sam and Al never made easy choices. Their path wasn't simple. They persevered and showed that it was possible to strive and succeed.

The hard work of Don, Deborah, Scott, Dean, and the rest of the QL crew gave us a new pair of heroes to look to when our lives become difficult. And a newfound strength to carry on.

Thanks, guys. We all miss you.

13

Stuff for Leapers

Newsletters/Letterzines:

Quantum Quarterly
c/o Jim Rondeau
1853 Fallbrook Ave.
San Jose, CA 95130

Newsletter, issues are $1.50 each, $6.00 for a four-issue subscription. Make checks payable to Jim Rondeau, indicate which issue you want your subscription to start with: 1–8.

The Imaging Chamber
c/o Catherine Woldow
Monte Cristo—Amethyst Press
6436 Simms St. #105
Arvada, CO 80004

Quarterly letterzine, 1–5 $1.50/issue, 6 on $4.50/issue. She will take multi-issue subscriptions. Issues: 1–8.

Leapin' In
Linda Cooksey
304 Bluff St.
Crawfordsville, IN 47933-1232

Monthly newsletter, single sheet, articles and
announcements. Subscription is $6 a year. Issues:
1–6.

Fiction Zines:

Accelerator Accidents
c/o Catherine Woldow
Monte Cristo—Amethyst Press
6436 Simms St. #105
Arvada, CO 80004

$20

Adventures in Slime and Time
Kathy Hintze
4646 NE Antioch Rd.
Kansas City, MO 64117

Ghostbusters and *QL*, $12.90

Faces of Clay
Ann Walton
4003 Old Hearne Rd.
Bryan, TX 77803

$12.50, 100 pp, is a cross-universe novel—
QL/*Crime Story*/with a little *Twin Peaks* thrown in—
very nice.

As Time Goes By
Mystery Frank (Mysti)
726 Zorn Ave. #2
Louisville, KY 40206

Green Eggs and Ham
Mystery Frank (Mysti)
726 Zorn Ave. #2
Louisville, KY 40206

$18.90, Another excellent zine from Mysti.

In Another Life, Pt 1
Martin Enterprises
PO Box 7669
McLean, VA 22106–7669

$14.95 + $3 US, $4 Canada postage.

Look Before You Leap
Michael Ruff—Ruff and Ready Press
110 Cedargrove Dr.
Rochester NY 14617

$12, 130pp.

A Matter of Time
Julie Barrett
Threadneedle Press
2624 E. Park Blvd.
Plano, TX 75074

#1, $10 by mail. Wonderful cover, excellent stories, if you want to try a zine, this is one of the top three to get. Number 2 is $11, with another nice cover, more fine stories, recycling tips, also planning a "chain" novel.

Oh Boy
Sandy Hall/Sharon Wisdom
4117 Comanche
Hannibal, MO 63401

Lots of good stuff. #1 ($16.50), #2 ($18). *Best of Two Worlds* ($5.50) is a novel sequel to "Second Circle" in Oh Boy #1. Sam has returned from leaping and decides to take a vacation a get a PhD in literature. (This came out in May '91, so it does not include the revelations in "The Leap Back.")

Out of the Blue
Penreddy Publishing
Kay Simon
P.O. Box 460658
Aurora, CO 80046-0658

Nice adventure stories, all original universes, some poetry, not illustrated. $14, 104pp.

Out of the Frying Pan
Sheila Paulson
2408 Beaver
Des Moines, IA 50310

$12.90 by mail. Sheila is a longtime writer, but this is her first zine, wonderful issue. Definitely an Al issue.

QL+ . . . #1
Darlene Fisher/Ann Teitelbaum
Almost Foolproof Press/Starlite Press
P.O. Box 2455
Danville, CA 94526

$7.50, 67pp, not illustrated. "Sam's Run"—Sam in *Logan's Run* universe (not too good).

Quantum Beast
Lee Kirkland
19211 E. Scott Place
Denver, CO 80249

Sam Beckett—Man About Time
Dapplewood Press
Sharon Wells
P.O. Box 9907
N. Hollywood, CA 91609-9907

#1 Quantum Jones: The Search for the Golden Doors ($12 + $3 postage); #2 Star Leap ($14 + $3), overdue (summer 91). #3 Double O Sam

Quantum Mechanics
Datazine Publications
P.O. Box 19413
Denver, CO 80219

Six stories by Jessica Farrow, $12.95, 62pp.

Play It Again
Kate Nuernberg
6713 Schroeder Rd #2
Madison, WI 53711

$12 + $3 postage. Very nice, somewhat darker in tone. #2 planned for 5/92.

With Every Quantum Leap and Bound
Melissa Wilson/Joseph Young
10675 Mathieson St.
San Diego, CA 92129

$12, delayed due to moving and computer problems

Clubs:

Project Quantum Leap
Karen Blocher, Project Chairman
P.O. Box 77513
Tucson, AZ 85703

$15/year, newsletter—The Observer #1–4

Quantum League
James McNair
19 Millburn Dr.
Etobicoke, Ontario, Canada M9B 2W8

$15/year, newsletter—The Newsleaguer, meets monthly

T-shirts

Creation
145 Jericho Turnpike
Mineola, NY 11501

Three designs: black T-shirt with the logo in pink or blue; a white T-shirt with a picture in blue and green of Sam and Al and scenes from different years like in the opening credits; a white T-shirt with a picture of Sam in orange and red. Price each—$13.98 + $2.00 postage.

Ashton Press
Ann Wortham
1402 Allison Ave.
Altamonte Springs, FL 32701

T-shirt with art by Leah Rosenthal (zine illustrator, coauthor of *Bizarro* and regular cartoonist in *Starlog*), "Who's Sam This Time?" (Sam as the fourth Doctor), $14, XXL $16, loads of colors (I got bright orange), write to Ann for details. Also a tote bag with the same picture, $13.

Comic Books

Innovation Corp.
3622 Jacob St.
Wheeling, WV 26003

The *QL* comic book, twelve issues planned, mail
order at $3 per issue.

☰ HarperAudio *By Mail*

If STAR TREK® MEMORIES
left you wanting more,
HarperAudio has the answer.

In October, **STAR TREK® MOVIE MEMORIES**, the sequel to the bestselling **STAR TREK® MEMORIES**, will be available. It details all the behind-the-scenes shenanigans in the making of the six Star Trek® movies. It also features on-the-set reporting from the filming of the seventh movie, coming to theaters in November, 1994. Like the audio of the first title, the sequel will be read by William Shatner, Capt. James T. Kirk, himself!

Order today to ensure that the tape of **STAR TREK® MOVIE MEMORIES** is sent to you as soon as it is available. While you're at it, get a copy of the **STAR TREK® MEMORIES** as well. That way, you'll have the complete collection.

If you can't wait until October to hear more from your favorite Star Trek® stars, order **WILLIAM SHATNER AND LEONARD NIMOY READ FOUR SCIENCE FICTION CLASSICS**. Here Shatner and Nimoy read four of science fiction's most mesmerizing tales. *Foundation: The Prehistorians* by Isaac Asimov and *Mimsy Were the Borogoves* by Henry Kunter are narrated by Shatner, while Nimoy reads *The Martian Chronicles* by Ray Bradbury and *The Green Hills of Earth* by Robert A. Heinlein. It is a collection every science fiction buff will want to listen to again and again.

The tapes are terrific entertainment anywhere. Pop them into your car stereo, plug in your headphones, or listen while at home—these fabulous tales will intrigue and entertain you for hours!

— — — — — — — — — — — — —

ORDER TODAY!
MAIL TO: HarperCollins Publishers
P.O. Box 588, Dunmore, PA 18512-0588
TELEPHONE: 1-800-331-3761 (Visa/Mastercard)

Yes, please send me the audios indicated below:

____**Star Trek® Memories** • 1-55994-783-7, $22.50
      4 cassettes, 4.5 hours, abridged
____**Star Trek® Movie Memories** • 0-69451-480-2, $22.50
      4 cassettes, approx. 6 hours, abridged
      (available 10/94)
____**William Shatner and Leonard Nimoy Read Four**
      Science Fiction Classics • 1-55994-884-1, $25.00
      4 cassettes, 4 hours, abridged

SUBTOTAL..._____
POSTAGE AND HANDLING.. 2.50_____
SALES TAX (Add applicable sales tax)........................._____
TOTAL..._____
(Remit in U.S. dollars, do not send cash.)

Name_____

Address_____

City_____ State_____ Zip_____

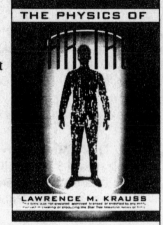